Leonard Doohan

The Contemporary Challenge Of John of the Cross
An Introduction to
His Life and Teaching

About the Author

Leonard Doohan is a professor of religious studies at Gonzaga University, Spokane, WA, where he teaches courses in biblical theology, laity in the church, and spirituality. He is also Dean of the Graduate School. He has given workshops throughout the United States, Canada, Australia, New Zealand, Europe, and several countries of the Far East. Dr. Doohan has written fourteen books, his latest on the Acts of the Apostles. *He regularly teaches a course and offers workshops on John of the Cross and Teresa of Avila, and has published several articles on John and audio tapes on both saints.*

Leonard Doohan

The Contemporary Challenge Of John of the Cross

An Introduction to His Life and Teaching

With a Preface by Ernest Larkin, O.Carm.

ICS Publications
Institute of Carmelite Studies
Washington, D.C.
1995

CA
248.237
D

ICS Publications
2131 Lincoln Road NE
Washington, DC 20002–1199

Typeset and produced in the U.S.A.

Dedication

*For my wife Helen on our anniversary
and for our daughter Eve-Anne on her graduation
with all my love*

Library of Congress Cataloging-in-Publication Data

Doohan, Leonard.
    The contemporary challenge of John of the Cross:
an introduction to his life and teaching / Leonard Doohan;
with a preface by Ernest Larkin, O.Carm.
      p.   cm.
    Includes bibliographical references.
    ISBN: 0–935216–55–3
    1. John, of the Cross, Saint, 1542–1591.
2. Christian saints—Spain—Biography . I. Title.
BX4700.J7D64   1994
271'.7302—dc20   94–41294
    [B]   CIP

TABLE OF CONTENTS

ABBREVIATIONS

Unless otherwise noted, all quotations from **St. John of the Cross** are taken from *The Collected Works of St. John of the Cross,* trans. Kieran Kavanaugh and Otilio Rodriguez, rev. ed. (Washington, DC: ICS Publications, 1991). For his major works, the following abbreviations are used:

A = Ascent of Mount Carmel
C = Spiritual Canticle
F = Living Flame of Love
N = Dark Night

In references to the *Ascent* and *Night,* the first number indicates the book. Also, references to John's *Poems, Letters,* and *Sayings* are based on the numbering of the cited text in this revised Kavanaugh/ Rodriguez translation, which sometimes differs from that of other editions. Thus, for example, "A, 1, 2, 3" refers to the third section of the second chapter in Book One of the *Ascent of Mount Carmel,* and "C, 4, 5" to the fifth section of the commentary on the fourth stanza in the *Spiritual Canticle.* Finally, when mentioned in the text, quotation marks are used for the titles of John's poems, and italics for the titles of his major treatises. Thus "Spiritual Canticle" refers to John's poem that begins "Where have you hidden," while *Spiritual Canticle* refers to his commentary on this poem.

ACKNOWLEDGMENTS

Thanks are due to Sr. Vilma Seelaus, O.C.D., and Sr. Leslie Lund, Carmelite Sister of Mary, who read the manuscript and offered helpful criticisms and suggestions, and to Fr. Ernest Larkin, O.Carm., who not only read the manuscript, making recommendations, but kindly agreed to write the preface. I wish also to thank Fr. Steven Payne, O.C.D., of ICS Publications, for his editorial work, and especially Fr. Frederico Ruiz, O.C.D., whose writings on John of the Cross have been the most significant influence in my own understanding of John's life and teachings. This book is the fruit of fourteen years of lecturing on John, interacting with participants' questions, and delving further into some of my own. I am also grateful to the many participants in my courses for their contributions.

CHRONOLOGY OF MAJOR DATES IN THE LIFE OF JOHN OF THE CROSS

1542 Birth of Juan de Yepes at Fontiveros, near Avila.

c. 1543 Death of John's father, Gonzalo de Yepes, and his brother, Luis. John's mother, Catalina, in search of work, decides to move the family to Arévalo, and later to Medina del Campo.

c. 1552–6 John goes to school at the Colegio de los Niños de la Doctrina, in Medina.

c. 1556–7 At the invitation of Don Alonso Alvarez de Toledo, John moves to Plague Hospital where he works as a nurse and continues his studies.

c. 1559–63 John attends the College of the Society of Jesus at Medina.

1563 John takes the Carmelite habit at St. Anne's, Medina del Campo, as Juan de San Matías.

1564 John makes his profession in the same priory, in Medina del Campo. Enters the University of Salamanca to study the arts and theology.

1565 On January 6, the feast of the Epiphany, John is among ten Carmelite students who matriculate at the University of Salamanca.

1567   John ordained as a priest. While at home in Medina
        for first Mass John meets Teresa of Avila, who is mak-
        ing a foundation there and searching for friars for
        the reform of the male branch of Carmel. She inter-
        views John in September or October. In November,
        John returns to the University of Salamanca to con-
        tinue his studies of theology.

1568   John spends part of his vacation at Medina del
        Campo. In August, he accompanies Teresa to
        Valladolid. In September, he returns to Medina and
        later goes to Avila and Duruelo. On November 28,
        John takes the vows of the Reform at Duruelo, to-
        gether with Antonio de Heredia (Antonio de Jesús),
        prior of the Carmelites at Medina, and José de Cristo,
        another Carmelite from Medina. John takes the sub-
        title "of the Cross" at this time.

1570   On June 11, the first community of the Reform
        moves from Duruelo to Mancera de Abajo. Some-
        time after October, John is sent to Pastrana as novice
        master. After spending about a month there, he re-
        turns to Mancera.

1571   Perhaps in April, John goes to Alcalá de Henáres as
        rector of the College of the Reform, and while there
        he directs the Carmelite nuns.

1572   John goes to Avila as confessor to the convent of the
        Incarnation and remains there till 1577.

1575–6 During the winter, John is kidnapped by the
        Carmelites and imprisoned at Medina del Campo.
        He is later freed by the intervention of the Papal
        Nuncio, Ormaneto.

1577   On the night of December 2, John is kidnapped by
        the Carmelites and carried off to the Carmelite

priory at Avila. After a short time he is taken prisoner to the priory at Toledo.

1577–8   In the Toledo prison, John begins writing poetry to express his inner spirit and for his own consolation.

1578   Sometime in August, perhaps the 16th or shortly thereafter, John escapes to the convent of the discalced Carmelite nuns in Toledo. In October, John attends a meeting of the discalced superiors at Almodóvar. They decide to send him to El Calvario as Vicar.

1578–9   During his time at El Calvario as Vicar, John goes weekly to the convent of Beas to hear confessions, and also during this period, he begins his commentary entitled *Ascent of Mount Carmel.*

1579   John founds a college of the Reform at Baeza and remains as rector for the next three years. During this time he continues his ministry of the written word.

1580   Death of John's mother.

1581   John attends the Alcalá Chapter of the Reform, arriving on March 3 or 4. He is appointed third definitor and prior of the Granada house of Los Mártires. In November John meets with St. Teresa in Avila. This was to be their last meeting.

1582   Toward the end of January, John arrives at Los Mártires in Granada. He is elected prior, visits the Beas convent occasionally and continues his writing—including the last five stanzas of the "Spiritual Canticle" poem (with it commentary), the finishing touches on the *Ascent of Mount Carmel,* and the whole of the *Living Flame of Love.*

1585   In May, the Lisbon Chapter appoints John second definitor and vicar-provincial of Andalusia.

1585–7 During these years, John makes the following foundations: Málaga, February, 1585; Córdoba, May, 1586; La Manchuela (de Jaén), October, 1586; Caravaca, December, 1586; Bujalance, June, 1587.

1587   In April, the chapter of Valladolid re-appoints John prior of Los Mártires.

1588   In August, John attends the chapter of the Reform in Madrid, and is elected first definitor. Later that month, John takes up his new role as prior of Segovia, the house that would become the headquarters for the government of the Reform. John acts as deputy for Fr. Doria, during the latter's absences.

1590   In June, John is reelected first definitor at the extraordinary chapter held in Madrid.

1591   On June 1, the eve of Pentecost, the general chapter opens in Madrid. John is left without office and sent to La Peñuela to prepare for assignment to Mexico. He arrives at La Peñuela in August. Within a few weeks, John falls victim to severe fever. On September 22 he leaves La Peñuela for Ubeda. John of the Cross dies at Ubeda on December 14th.

1675   Beatified by Clement X on January 25.

1726   Canonized by Benedict XIII on December 27.

1577   Declared Doctor of the Church Universal by Pius XI on August 24.

PREFACE

This book provides a clear and comprehensive framework for the serious student of St. John of the Cross. It is a doctrinal introduction; it maps out the territory, setting down the goal, the stages, and the way one advances in the journey to God. The book is a contemporary challenge, because John's doctrine is addressed with an eye on today's humanistic and social viewpoints.

Two preliminary chapters present the man and the poetry. This is essential background for the study of the doctrine. The importance of the search for the true humanity of John and the function of the poetry as the primary revelation of his experience are givens in contemporary Sanjuanist studies. Professor Doohan gives careful attention to both topics.

The gradual retrieval of the saint's authentic personality and a better appreciation of the poetry are ongoing gains from recent studies. More remains to be done, especially on the biography, because John will be heard today only insofar as he is perceived as an attractive human being of great sensitivity and feeling, and not as an ethereal, austere figure who falls out of heaven.

The poetry brings out these qualities. It is also a more adequate expression of the mystical experience than the discursive prose, which after all only attempts to unpack the poetry. For this reason, readers today are urged to return to the poetry over and over again. Without the poetry the commentaries are in danger of becoming fossilized.

The targeted audience for John's writings are not beginners in the spiritual life. John in fact has little to say to them; his concern is to lead beginners as quickly as possible into the full life of the Spirit, which is contemplation. This path alone leads to divine union, which is the ultimate goal of all his direction. John is "a specialist in the later stages of the spiritual life" (p. 63).

The famous diagram of "The Mount of Perfection" portrays divine union as the center path that alone leads to the top of Mount Carmel; two imperfect ways of the Christian life (the so-called "sweet and delectable ways") meander around the foothills. Both imperfect ways, one religious, the other secular, represent a divided heart and do not lead to the fullness of union with God.

One is placed on the center path by "choice-oriented love," which by intention is total, exclusive, and absolute. This love is distinguished from a love that grows bit by bit, through an "accumulation" of scattered acts. Choice-love is bent on integrating all other loves into the one movement into God. The goal is to bring one's whole life under the movement of charity. This is a liberating, contemporary insight into the categories of spirit and sense in John, which too often are interpreted in a dualistic, platonic fashion.

"Spiritual" and "spirit "are terms John uses to describe the *whole* person directed to God, whereas the sensual person ("sense") short-circuits the movement to God and settles for some part of life. It does not matter whether that part is a religious or secular feature, since in both cases the person ends up in the same dead end. What does matter for John of the Cross is that God be *All* in all. God is *Nothing* as well, nothing of creation, hence the necessity of total human emptiness or freedom from all things. The paradox of this mystical truth is that the God-centered life is the fullness of human life.

The spiritual journey is the cultivation of choice-love. Professor Doohan presents the journey in the framework of the three traditional ways of beginners, proficients, and the perfect, but with a difference. The difference is the role assigned to the two purifying dark nights of sense and of spirit.

These dark nights are the trademark of St. John of the Cross. Professor Doohan gives them a new twist by explaining them as distinct stages of growth, sandwiched between the classical three ways.

They are the periods of real growth, the night of sense occurring between the beginnings and proficiency, the night of spirit after proficiency. Proficiency itself is a state of relative rest and consolidation between two dynamic periods of growth. There are thus five stages along the way. The nights themselves are two degrees of the one same night of purification. The first night deals with the symptoms and cuts off the branches of human limitation and sinfulness; the second night pulls up the roots of the obstacles.

The journey is the progressive assimilation of the gift of God, received in ever purer faith, hope, and love. This theological life is the constant perspective of John of the Cross. This fact puts John's teaching at the very heart of the church, available for believers of all vocations and states of life who yearn for the inner renewal of life called for by Vatican II.

This excellent work opens up the treasures of John of the Cross for our contemporaries. We are indebted to Professor Doohan for the years of research and teaching that made this book possible. We congratulate him and wish his book a wide circulation.

Ernest E. Larkin, O.Carm.
Kino Institute, Phoenix, Arizona

Map of Spain

FRANCE

Galicia

Asturias

Old Castille

Leon

Catalan

Aragon

PORTUGAL

Medina del Campo

Salamanca

Segovia

Avila

MADRID

Pastrana

New Castille

Toledo

Extremadura

Valencia

LISBON

Almodóvar del Campo

Beas

Murcia

Baeza

Ubeda

Andalusia

Seville

Granada

Principal Sites Associated with
St. John of the Cross

John's Early Years

John's Final Years

INTRODUCTION

While in the last stages of writing this book, my family and I were invited to Spain. Although I had traveled throughout northern Spain and visited Segovia and Avila on various occasions, I had never before been to southern Spain. I planned a personal pilgrimage to several of the places associated with John of the Cross.

My wife and I first passed through Málaga where John had founded a house of the reform in 1585, and on to Granada where we arrived early in the morning. After a cup of coffee, we visited the convent of Discalced Carmelite nuns in the center of the city, just a couple of minutes from the great Cathedral and Royal Chapel of the Catholic Monarchs, Ferdinand and Isabella. Mother Superior and two sisters received us with much kindness, giving me lots of time to ask about places and events in Granada connected with John's stay there from 1582 to 1588. The sisters showed us relics of John, a walking stick he used in his frequent trips from his monastery of Los Mártires to the convent for confessions and spiritual direction, and some documents in John's own hand. The latter were especially interesting, and one of the sisters pointed out that John's signature had been cut out of the documents, probably for devotional reasons.

On January 20, 1582, John officiated at the opening of the house in Granada, and the first superior had been Ana de Jesús (Anne of Jesus), whom John had met in Mancera in 1570, when Mother Teresa passed through the town with a group of sisters on her way to Salamanca and then to Valladolid to found a new convent. Mother Anne of Jesus did us all a great service by asking John to explain the "Spiritual Canticle" poem; John did so, dedicating the

1

commentary to her. The sisters were evidently proud of the fact that John had founded their convent in Granada and excited to share their history. However, it was equally clear that what they valued most of all was the life and spirit of the reform that they sought to prolong in their own lives.

Overlooking Granada is the great fortress of the Alhambra, and on the southern slopes of the hill on which it is built are the ruins of Los Mártires, the monastery of the Carmelite reform that John saw for the first time in 1582. It is called Los Mártires because tradition commemorates there the martyrdom of twelve Christians by the Moors. Here John built his hermitage, in what is now a ruined and overgrown section closed to the general public. My wife and I arrived after a long walk from the city center in the heat of a Granada early afternoon, retracing John's steps. We saw a guide to the museum just getting into his car to go home, but when I mentioned my interest in John of the Cross he excitedly got out of his car and spent over an hour showing us all around the grounds of what was once an early house of the reform. Señor Paco Morente was a government tour guide. He informed us that he had little interest in the museum, but that his heart was always in the history and influence of John of the Cross. Señor Morente, whom friends appropriately called El Sereno, showed us the small lake with its old ruined tower where tradition suggested the twelve were martyred, their throats cut. He pointed out the twelve columns, symbolizing the martyred group, and reminded us of John's desire that the little lake area be kept as a shrine. An aqueduct designed and built by John still provides the lake's water.

It was sad to see the grounds, buildings, and gardens so neglected. The whole surroundings on the lower slopes of the Alhambra hill were quite barren, with most of the trees cut down. Once this area must have been quite beautiful, and even today it evokes memories of the Mystical Doctor; it was here that John finished the *Ascent of Mount Carmel,* wrote the *Dark Night of the Soul* (1582-84), added eight stanzas and wrote his commentary to the "Spiritual Canticle" poem (1584), and composed both the poem and commentary on the *Living Flame of Love* (1585).

Our second day of journeying with John of the Cross again began very early. Our goal was Ubeda, where John died. However, we first stopped in Baeza, where John had opened a house of studies for the friars close to the old university. There he resided from 1579-82. In Baeza, John wrote part of "En una noche oscura" (the "Dark Night" poem), and some of the *Ascent of Mount Carmel*. Some commentators think he may also have written several later verses of the "Spiritual Canticle" poem here and completed a section of the commentary.

When we arrived, several shopkeepers were preparing for the day ahead, sweeping outside their stores. I asked directions to several places connected with John's life, and within a few minutes there was a small group of local people telling me enthusiastically about the history of their town and its connections with John. While not all their directions or history were accurate, it was delightful to share in their pride. We crossed the Plaza del Mercado Viejo, and met a Carmelite friar, much as villagers might have done four centuries ago as they encountered John going about his ministry. The friar, informed of our plans for the day, told us about John and places we "had to see." We visited the old university and the Cathedral built by Ferdinando III, "El Santo," who conquered the area in 1227; both buildings were standing in John's time. We saw the site of a convent that John visited to give spiritual direction, now a modern school of arts and sciences, and we saw more recent Carmels.

At the monastery of the Discalced Carmelite friars in Ubeda, we entered their museum of the life and times of John through the same door through which John of the Cross was brought on September 28, 1591, suffering from fever and inflammation of his leg. John suffered much in those days in Ubeda, and died peacefully at midnight on December 14, 1591.

The museum contains the room where John died, the table on which his body was prepared for burial, the chapel where his funeral took place and where he was briefly buried from his death in 1591 to May 1593, when his body was transferred to Segovia, Elsewhere the museum shows episodes from John's life, using the actual items associated with John whenever possible, such as a table where he sat to give direction. There are also relics, writings of John, artistic portrayals of his life and teachings, and art and books inspired by John. It was both a fascinating and a moving experience for us; enriched by the kindness and dedication of our friar-guide.

We left the monastery and paused to get a drink at a bar in the square next to the Church of St. Paul's where John's statue now stands. Struggling to remember a word in Spanish, I exclaimed to the bar owner how difficult it was dealing with everyone in a language not your own. To which he replied "Nothing is difficult when people treat you well." I remember his words as a fine ending to a special morning; I could not help recalling how John in his last days had won over the abusive prior of Ubeda by treating him well, after Fr. Crisóstomo had treated him so poorly. "Where there is no love," John used to say, "put love, and there you will draw out love."

After Ubeda, we journeyed through the northern sections of Andalusia, passing several cities linked to John: Linares where he founded a convent, Andújar with its parish church where the autograph copy of the *Sayings of Light and Love* is kept. Our stay in Cordoba was brief, to see some of the sights he would have seen. We visited the beautiful cathedral and old city he would have known, and the modern convent and monastery that prolong his spirit.

The next morning we left early and soon found ourselves outside the cathedral in Seville, a city John visited in 1586 to help some nuns of the reform transfer to a new convent. The capital city of Andalusia, and the fourth largest city of Spain, Seville boasts an extraordinary history filled with great monarchs, soldiers, missionaries, philosophers, and theologians. We returned to the coast by way of Ronda, through the magnificent scenery of southwest Spain. We had traveled about a thousand kilometers in three days, had seen many of the foundations of John, and several places with special memories of his life, work, ministry, and last hours.

It was delightful to see how proud the Andalusians remain of their cities' associations with John, and to find that his work of reform endured in the poverty, simplicity, and dedication of the contempory people we met. It was particularly challenging to see the countryside that inspired his poetry. Whenever I now read John, I am reminded of the people, the places, and the images of the three days in Andalusia. Seeing how vital John's spirit and teaching remain even among the ordinary folk of southern Spain helped convince me again that John has a message for our time, not just for academics or members of contemplative religious orders, but for all those who seek God in an often confusing world.

CHAPTER ONE

The Life and Times of John of the Cross

Contemporary Relevance of John of the Cross

John of the Cross is a figure of prime importance in the history of Christian spirituality. Persecuted during his own life, ignored after his death, and frequently misrepresented as a hard, cold, inhuman person, John is appreciated today as one of the most healthily integrated individuals of the Christian tradition. Interest in John's teachings and appreciation of his extraordinary insights into Christian life and prayer are higher than ever and still growing. Even people who, at one time or another, have been put off by misrepresentations of John as harsh, still have the nagging conviction that John's understanding of Christian life is probably right, and sooner or later they will need to follow his lead.

John lived from 1542 to 1591 and was known principally for his work of the reform of Carmelite friars in Spain, a reform he undertook under the direction of Teresa of Avila. Along with his work as reformer, John was also well-known for his spiritual direction of nuns in the many communities that Teresa founded. Recognized as an intelligent student in his early years in Medina del Campo and Salamanca, he was later appreciated as a fine scholar by university faculties, at Baeza and elsewhere. However, he was not valued as an original thinker in his own day. In fact, theological originality was hardly what post-reformation Spain was looking for! John was usually considered a disciple of Thomas Aquinas and of the Areopagite.

Recognized during his life more as a saintly person than a prophet, John's influence was generally restricted to the Teresian Carmel, and limited even there, due to efforts of some of his own friars to humiliate and disgrace John in his last years.

The initial steps towards beatification began in 1614, twenty-three years after John's death, and the tensions between John and some supporters of Fr. Nicolás Doria (the superior of the discalced at the time John died) were still evident in the Carmelite superiors who wrote affidavits for the process. Moreover, John's writings were also receiving mixed responses, and some editors felt they needed a little doctoring up for the process. John was beatified by Clement X on January 25, 1675, and fifty years later was canonized by Benedict XIII on December 27, 1726.

In 1881, the Spanish scholar Marcelino Menéndez Pelayo, on the occasion of his solemn induction into the Academy of Language, gave an address on Spanish mystical poetry, in which he presented John of the Cross as the greatest poet of the Spanish language.[1] This brought John out of the shadows and into public view. In 1926, Pius XI declared John a *Doctor of the Universal Church,* and from then on his authority as a writer and theologian grew. Writers such as Jacques Maritain proposed that a systematic analysis of John's work justified giving him the title "the Mystical Doctor." French thinkers such as Bergson, Baruzi, and Morel studied John as a philosopher. The literary and artistic quality of John's poetry was critically defended by Dámaso Alonso in 1942.

A great poet, theologian, mystical doctor, philosopher, and literary genius, John is unquestionably one of the most balanced individuals among the Church's saints.

People today are impressed not only by John's extraordinary quality of expression but also by the purity and authenticity of his message. There is a ring of truth to his teaching, and people value his uncompromising search for union with God. While contemporary optimistic spiritualities may keep people going in the reasonably peaceful plateau periods, the same people often turn to John for guidance in the critical "dark nights" of life. John is not only a great mystic but an outstanding spiritual guide, who is still directing disciples today.

John also has many down-to-earth qualities that make him appealing today and show how mystical union can be part of our contemporary struggle-filled lives. When Teresa first met John in Medina del Campo she recognized not only the depth of his spiritual life, but his leadership abilities, too. When John went to open the first house of the Teresian reform in Duruelo, he showed his practical building and painting skills in remodeling the house. He was good at finances, too, and Teresa said that she and John had several arguments about the business side of their ventures. While serving as confessor at the Incarnation he sketched, and his picture of the crucified Christ became the basis for one of Salvador Dali's most famous paintings. When first taken prisoner in Avila, John was resourceful enough to escape briefly and go back to the Incarnation to destroy correspondence that could incriminate others. Although brutally treated by his own brothers in religious life, he managed not to become bitter. When imprisoned in Toledo for nine months, weak and hungry, he prudently planned a daring escape. In the provincial chapters of discalced friars, John was sometimes a lone voice against autocratic leadership, insisting on secret voting, and courageously defending others against oppression. He was spied on by his own associates, reported to authorities, and unjustly maligned. He took some of it with humor, but could always distinguish between issues and people. He was a good local superior, an able regional vicar, and an elected provincial councilor. Requested to open a new house, John could arrange the whole project—episcopal permissions, buildings, finance, local support, personnel—in a very short time, as he did in Baeza. When Fr. Doria needed a local superior for Segovia who could oversee the expansion of the residence and generate the necessary financial support for the development, he chose John. Once events turned against him again, John could assess things well and avoid awkward situations, as when he resisted going back as prior of Segovia, where he would have been in the middle of political disputes among the friars.

John was a great mystic who lived in deep union with God; yet at the same time he was a great practical reformer, builder, leader, director, and writer. His mysticism was not achieved through withdrawal from real life, but while struggling with unjust ecclesiastical pressures and persecutions. Besides an outstanding teacher, he was a wonderful model of uncompromising dedication to God and the life of prayer, amid the pressures of daily life.

Early Life of John of the Cross

Juan de Yepes was born in 1542 in Fontiveros, then a town of about 5,000 inhabitants, situated twenty-four miles northwest of Avila, on the Castilian plateau. John was the third child of Gonzalo de Yepes and Catalina Alvarez. Gonzalo came from a family of wealthy silk merchants, but his relatives disowned him when he married the poor orphaned girl, Catalina Alvarez, whose family (possibly of Moorish ancestry) originally came from Toledo. Not long after John's birth, Gonzalo died, after a prolonged, painful illness, leaving his young widow, Catalina, without the means to bring up her three sons; Francisco, Luis (who soon died, apparently of malnutrition), and the youngest, John, who was no more than a few years old. The family lived in poverty, in spite of the constant and heroic efforts of Catalina.[2] She first traveled to the province of Toledo, hoping her dead husband's brothers would help her children. One brother, a rich archdeacon, threw out his half-starved relatives; another, a doctor, kept one of the sons, but Francisco was so mistreated by the doctor's wife he rejoined his poor wandering family. They left Fontiveros in search of work and food, settling first in Arévalo for three years, and later in Medina del Campo, a Castilian town of about 30,000. The year was 1551, and John was nine years old.

Catalina shared a house with her eldest son, Francisco, now twenty one, and his wife, Ana Izquierdo. Catalina decided to send John to one of Medina's Catechism Schools, boarding schools where orphans learned a trade and were generally fed and clothed by the endowment of one of the city's wealthy, in this case Don Rodrigo de Dueñas Hormaza. John worked as a carpenter, tailor, and painter, without much success. Eventually Alonso Alvarez de Toledo, administrator of the Plague Hospital, took an interest in John, who moved from the Catechism School to the Hospital de la Concepción, one of fourteen hospitals in Medina. John showed both ability and interest in the hospital ministry, dedicating himself to the patients in loving service, and to the institution in begging alms for its support. At 17, while continuing his work at the hospital, John received Don Alonso's permission to begin a course of studies at the Jesuit College near the hospital. John could already read and write; his attendance at the "colegio" involved four years of serious training in the humanities. He was very successful at his school work and loved to study, a characteristic that would remain with him throughout his life.

John's family continued to struggle and, despite their poverty, were exemplary Christians, caring for many orphans and always ready to share the little they had with others less fortunate.

Many people in Medina respected John and offered him positions at the end of his studies. The administrator of Plague Hospital recommended John for ordination and offered him the position of chaplain. Others offered him employment, and religious orders invited him to join them. One day in 1563, unknown to those interested in his future, John entered the Carmelite monastery, where he would be known as Brother John of St. Matthias. After what seems to have been a happy novitiate year, John was professed and soon obtained permission to observe the Primitive Rule of the Order. John was sent to the college of San Andrés, a Carmelite house of studies in Salamanca. He arrived in 1564, already a good student, and he studied at the university under some of the outstanding scholars of the day, including Luis de León.[3] The University of Salamanca was in its glory, with a student body of nearly seven thousand. John was an excellent student, appointed prefect of students, but also known for his piety and austerity.[4]

At the end of his third year of theology, John went to Medina del Campo to celebrate his first Mass with his family. In the late summer of 1567, he met Mother Teresa of Avila, to whom John had been recommended as a possible leader in the reform of the friars.[5] Teresa had received authorization to establish two houses of her reform for the Carmelite friars from the Master General, Juan Bautista Rubeo (Rossi), visiting Spain to encourage the reforms of the Council of Trent. John told Teresa he was considering transferring to the Carthusians, but she insisted that his desires for contemplation and penance could be fulfilled in her reformed Carmel.

John returned to Salamanca, concluded his studies, and was back in Medina by the summer of 1568. That July, Teresa arrived to encourage John and Antonio de Heredia to start the first reformed monastery for Carmelite friars in Duruelo, in a dilapidated farm house that Teresa had received from a benefactor in Avila. When permissions were obtained, John set out from Valladolid, where he had been helping Teresa with a new foundation, and where, she writes, "there was an opportunity to teach [him] about our way of life so that he would have a clear understanding of everything, whether it concerned mortification or the style of both our community life and the recreation we have together" (*Foundations,* 13, 5). After this "second novitiate" at Teresa's hands, instead of going directly to Duruelo John went to Avila. There he spent some time with a layman, Francisco de Salcedo, one of the readers of Teresa's original autobiography, and a person she trusted.

When John left Avila for Duruelo he was accompanied by a stonemason, who helped in remodelling the old building that was to become the first monastery of the reformed friars. About two months after their arrival, on November 28, 1568, the First Sunday of Advent, John (now "John of the Cross"), Antonio (now "Anthony of Jesus"), and José de Cristo formally renounced the mitigation of Eugene IV and dedicated themselves to the primitive rule of the Carmelites as approved by Innocent IV. Mother Teresa was to visit Duruelo in the following March, and was delighted at the spirit she found. This first monastery of friars served the Teresian reform for only a year and a half, by which time it was already too small; it was abandoned on June 11, 1570, when the friars transferred to Mancera de Abajo, three miles away.

John of the Cross and Teresa of Avila

John met Teresa for the first time in 1567; she was fifty-two and he twenty-five. Teresa's great conversion took place in 1554, and she founded the first house of her reform at St. Joseph's in Avila, in 1563. When she met John, she was already a woman of spiritual stature in Castile, who had written the second version of her autobiography in 1565, and the *Way of Perfection* in 1566. She was seeking promising candidates for a new community of Carmelite friars who would live according to the same spirit as the nuns of her Teresian Reform.

Their initial conversation in Medina de Campo focused on plans for John's involvement in Teresa's reform of the friars, but John must have kept this secret from his Carmelite superiors. Teresa had discussed her plans with at least two other Carmelite friars without finding the leadership she wanted. At this first meeting Teresa concluded John was the person she sought.[6]

They met again in July 1568, at which time the plans to open the monastery at Duruelo were finalized.[7] After Teresa's first meeting with John, she rejoiced; and when she sent John to stay awhile with Francisco de Salcedo, she could say of John: "we have never seen an imperfection in him." Teresa was a strong-willed individual, but John, too, was both courageous and firm in his opinions. In fact, Teresa acknowledges their disagreements in business matters, and confesses being annoyed with John on several occasions. He was intensely committed to the reform, starting the new life as soon as he arrived in Duruelo, a fact that disappointed Antonio de Heredia, who felt John should have waited for him. When Teresa visited Duruelo in March, 1569, she warned the friars there against excesses in penance, but they did not decrease the intensity of their life.[8]

Teresa's second community of friars began with two hermits already living in Pastrana, who wished to join a religious order, following the encouragement of the Council of Trent. The monastery of San Pedro de Pastrana was officially established on July 13, 1569. As in Mancera, novices came to Pastrana, and their formation became a critical issue, especially since (unlike John) the original two hermits were not steeped in the Teresian spirit. John of the Cross, the novice master in Mancera, was sent to Pastrana around the middle of October 1570 to organize the novitiate there. John stayed only a month, focusing on the essentials of the spirit of Carmel and preparing an acting novice master. By November, John was back in Mancera, where he met Teresa, who was on her way to Salamanca, accompanied by a group of sisters and one young novice, Anne of Jesus, to whom John would later dedicate the *Spiritual Canticle*.

In April 1571, John was chosen as rector of the discalced Carmelite house of studies in Alcalá de Henares, where his prime responsibility was the students' spiritual growth. Some accused John of encouraging excessive mortification, but the Apostolic commissioner, a Dominican, called to resolve the issue, was strong in his support of John and the quality of formation he was giving.[9] When, a short time later, John was asked to intervene in a dispute between frustrated novices in Pastrana and their excessive novice master, John, stressing that penance was a means and not the end of spiritual training, urged moderation, and was supported by both Teresa and the great theologian, Domingo Báñez.

In 1571, Teresa was appointed prioress of the convent of the Incarnation in Avila. She had entered the Carmel of the Incarnation in 1535, and spent 27 years there before inaugurating her reform. The original foundation inside the city walls of Avila had been intended for 14 *beatas;* later, a spacious new monastery was built outside the walls and the numbers rose to about 200 by 1565. A few years earlier, when Teresa made her first foundation of the reform, few nuns from the Incarnation were interested in accompanying her. "This Babylon," as Teresa referred to the Incarnation in a letter to her friend Doña Luisa de la Cerda, included many women who did not want to be there, but whose families were unable to find suitable husbands or provide marriage dowries.

Now 56 years old, Teresa was escorted by the Carmelite provincial, the mayor of Avila, some of the city police, and several curious onlookers who expected an entertaining event. The provincial, finding the main door barred, tried to enter through the choir but was blocked again by disgruntled nuns, claiming their canonical rights to elect a prioress. Meanwhile, some of Teresa's supporters intoned the *Te Deum.* The noise of 130 protesting nuns could be heard from the city walls, half a mile away!

The first weeks were oppressive for Teresa, who also became quite ill. She requested that John of the Cross should be appointed confessor to the Incarnation. The request was not without problems; the nuns as the Incarnation were not part of the Teresian reform, not "discalced" like Teresa and John, nor were the previous Carmelite chaplains. Moreover, Teresa's own tumultuous arrival was still fresh in people's minds. The apostolic commissary took the risk and appointed John vicar for the Incarnation; John and another "discalced" friar, along with some friars of the nearby Carmelite monastery, were to serve as confessors for the nuns. Eventually John became, along with Teresa, one of the two principal spiritual guides of the Incarnation, and by the end of 1572 peace and renewal were coming to the convent.[10]

At various times in her life, Teresa had consulted several spiritual directors. The two reformers were together in Avila for several years and Teresa greatly valued John's direction. In 1572 Teresa attained the fullness of the mystical life, reaching the state of "mystical marriage," generally thought to have begun on November 18, 1572, as John gave her communion. While at the Incarnation, John's reputation as spiritual guide grew, and others outside the convent entrusted extremely difficult discernment cases to him.

John was in his early thirties, but already a theologian, reformer, novice master, rector, confessor, exorcist, and visionary. The Lord continued to enrich John's mature spiritual life with deeper experiences, some of which he narrated to others, as when he gave Sister Ana María de Jesús an ink sketch of Christ crucified, the result of a vision. There are documents describing several occasions of deep faith-sharing between John and Teresa.

John made several short journeys while based in Avila, one of them to Segovia to open a new convent on March 19, 1574. Although the initial experience ended in an unpleasant clash with the vicar general of the diocese, who had not been informed of her foundation (though the bishop had given oral permission), Segovia was eventually to be intimately connected with John of the Cross, and his tomb is there today.

The Enemies of Reform

Reform and renewal always have their enemies: the constant power of evil, well-intentioned people who are misinformed or unwilling to change, men and women who gain power from religion and are reluctant to let it go, and—perhaps most insidiously—those whose apparent reforming zeal masks self-interested motives. Not everyone was enthusiastic about the Teresian Carmelite reform; both Teresa and John had their critics and opponents. Many alarming rumors circulated about what the "discalced" were up to, and not all of Teresa's followers always behaved admirably.

During the reform there were not only clashes between the new "discalced" Carmelites and their parent order (the "primitive" and "ancient" observances of Carmel, respectively)[11] but conflicts among Roman, Imperial, and Carmelite authorities. The Carmelite prior general, Father Rubeo, had begun a general visitation of the Spanish provinces in 1566. After meeting Teresa at San José in 1567, he had enthusiastically endorsed further Teresian foundations, eventually giving Teresa added permission to establish two communities of friars. In 1567, without the consent of the Carmelite General, Philip II obtained the brief *Superioribus mensibus* entrusting the reform of the Carmelites to the local bishops. When this approach proved unsuccessful, the pope then entrusted the visitation of the Carmelites to two Observant Dominicans: Pedro Fernández for Castile, and Francisco Vargas for Andalusia. The former prudently worked in collaboration with the Carmelite provincial of Castile; the latter ignored Carmelite authorities and imposed his own reformers. The Spanish provinces, angered by Vargas's treatment, urged their general to petition Rome for freedom from external visitations and for the appointment of Carmelites as visitators. Gregory XIII granted these requests in a brief of August 13, 1574, placing the visitation in the hands of the prior general and his delegates, but this response was not immediately made public in Spain.

The papal nuncio to Spain, Nicolás Ormaneto, was a firm ally of the reform. Informed of Gregory XIII's decision, but reassured by the papal secretary that his own authority as nuncio to visit and reform religious orders remained intact, Ormaneto, on his own initiative, reappointed the two previous visitators, Fernandez and Vargas. He gave them even greater authority, and added a third reformer, Jerónimo Gracían, for the province of Andalusia. Gracián was a close friend of Teresa, and a leader in the reform.

Matters came to a head in May 1575, at the Carmelite General Chapter held in Piacenza, Italy. Rossi (Rubeo) had written twice to Teresa, asking for explanations regarding the reform, but she did not receive the correspondence until June, and her silence in the meantime was interpreted as rebellion. Moreover, the discalced had no one to speak for them at the Chapter, since even the delegates from Castile and Andalusia, some of whom might have addressed the problem of the reform more dispassionately (or at least more knowledgeably), were absent when the Chapter opened. The Chapter approved a number of resolutions, such as: 1) There was to be one visitator for both branches of Carmel; 2) houses of the reform founded without the General's permission (mostly in Andalusia) were to be suppressed, and new houses were forbidden; 3) the Carmelites of the reform were not to attempt to form a separate province; 4) they were not to be called "discalced" but "contemplatives" or "primitives"; and 5) Teresa was to retire to a convent of her choice and be confined there.

In mid-1576, the general visitator appointed by Rossi, Jerónimo Tostado, arrived in Spain, but both king and nuncio rejected his authority, and he withdrew to Portugal. In September of the same year, relying on his authority as apostolic visitator by appointment of the papal nuncio Ormaneto, Gracián attempted to found a separate discalced province, and convoked a meeting, or chapter, in Almodóvar del Campo. During this chapter, John defended the importance of the contemplative dimension of the Carmelite life, and the need to safeguard it. The Almodóvar Chapter decided to send representatives to Rome to lobby for the reform; they also directed John of the Cross (probably at his own suggestion) to resign from the chaplaincy at the Incarnation, since this was a sore point with the "calced" friars of Avila. In fact, their prior had forcefully removed John in December 1575, sending him to the monastery in Medina del Campo, a public scandal only terminated with the firm intervention of the nuncio. In spite of Almodóvar, John did not leave the Incarnation, since Ormaneto had reconfirmed him in his post.

Those Carmelites not belonging to the Teresian reform were angered by the meeting at Almodóvar, and events moved in their favor when the nuncio, Ormaneto, died on June 18, 1577, and was replaced by Felipe Sega, a supporter of the "calced." The discalced expected the worst. Sometime during the night between December 3 and 4, the Incarnation was attacked by armed men, including friars and lay supporters, under the direction of the prior of Toledo, Fr. Hernando Maldonado. They broke down the door, seized John and his companion, bound them and led them off to the Carmelite monastery, where they were whipped twice. On the second day of his imprisonment, John slipped past his guard and returned to the

Incarnation to destroy documents that could have proved incrimi-
nating to members of the reform, before being recaptured. It was
decided to take John secretly to Toledo. John, now thirty-five, was
sick and weak, but rejected friendly offers to help him escape. John's
captors made him travel blindfolded and took him in a roundabout
way, along back roads, arriving finally at the Carmelite monastery in
Toledo.

John was brought before the tribunal of Tostado, the visitator,
who threatened, cajoled, and even tried to bribe John to reject the
reform and submit to the decisions of the Chapter of Piacenza. John
refused, confident that the discalced had been acting under the
higher authority of the papal nuncio. For this he was declared a
rebel and placed in the official monastery prison. After two months,
when it became known that John's companion had escaped, John
was transferred to another cell specially prepared for him. Originally a lavatory for the adjoining guest room, it was about nine by
five feet, with only a loophole three fingers wide, high up in the wall,
to give light. John's bed was nothing more than a board on the floor
and two old blankets. Dressed only in the tunic of his habit, and left
only his breviary to read, John was imprisoned for nearly nine
months, weak from illness, deprived of all liturgy, suffering from
hunger, frostbite in winter, searing heat in summer, and profound
abandonment. Monday, Wednesday, and Friday he was given only
bread and water. On Wednesdays every member of the community
joined in a communal public lashing of John. He was not allowed to
wash and never given a change of clothes in the first six months he
was there.

During this time no one among the discalced knew where
John was, and although some friars in the Toledo monastery, especially companions from the student years in Salamanca, admired
John, they were strictly bound to silence and unable to support
him.[12]

After six months, a friar assigned as John's new warden gave
him clean clothes and writing material. Once August came, John
began planning his escape, convinced this was his only chance of
ever leaving alive. His daring escape reads like a spy-thriller. Lower-
ing himself from a window in the corridor outside his cell, he made
his way through the unfamiliar city of Toledo by night, hid in the

cloister of the discalced Carmelite nuns' convent, and was later transferred secretly to the private quarters of Pedro González de Mendoza, administrator of the Hospital of Santa Cruz. From the safety of his room John could see the window through which he had escaped.[13]

The whole story of John's imprisonment may shock us today, but we need to recall the very complicated interplay between various levels of authority: papal, imperial, congregational, and local. The climate of post-reformation Spain also led to intrareligious conflict. John's treatment followed the practice of the period for dealing with religious regarded as disobedient. Moreover, if those who opposed the Teresian reform are criticized here, the discalced acted no better toward Gracián, who was eventually welcomed and cared for by the friars of the ancient observance.

John's Persecutions Among the Discalced

Two months after John's escape, at the beginning of October 1578, the discalced held another Chapter at Almodóvar, at which Anthony of Jesus was elected provincial of the attempted discalced province, and John was chosen superior of El Calvario. When the nuncio Sega learned of these actions, he declared them null and void, imprisoned several of the delegates and excommunicated all who participated in the Almodóvar chapter.

But John was already making his way to El Calvario in Andalusia, where he was to become prior of an exemplary community of about 30 friars. On Saturdays, he would go to the convent at Beas as spiritual director, and on other days compose and edit some of his writings. In the spring of 1579, the faculty of the University of Baeza made it known that they wanted a college for Carmelite students, and John responded, opening the house on June 13, celebrating the first Mass there the following day, Trinity Sunday, and becoming the first rector.[14]

On June 22, 1580, with the apostolic letter *Pia consideratione*, Gregory XIII granted the request for the discalced to become a separate province. This was partly the result of much discussion between Philip II and the nuncio, Sega, the latter eventually reversing his former opposition to the idea. The discalced convened their

first official provincial chapter on March 3, 1581, in Alcalá de
Henares. The Chapter elected Gracián as provincial and John as
one of four definitors, or councilors (responsible for assisting the
provincial in overseeing the members' fidelity to the *Constitutions*).

Still rector of Baeza, John made a few short journeys on the
Order's work, but in November 1581, Gracián gave John a pleasant
assignment to return to Avila to discuss a new foundation for
Granada with Mother Teresa. It was the first time John had seen
Teresa since the horrors of his imprisonment, four years earlier, and
the last time before Teresa's death the following year. Teresa gave
her encouragement, but declined to make the foundation in person; John then took great interest in helping Anne of Jesus and the
Carmelite nuns to establish the convent. He remained in Granada
as the newly elected prior of the friars' monastery there.

In May 1583, the discalced again held a chapter at Almodóvar,
where the tension between Gracián's emphasis on apostolate and
Doria's on contemplation surfaced yet again. In the spring of 1585,
another chapter was held, this time in Lisbon, and Gracián nomi-
nated Doria for provincial. This turned out to be an unfortunate
move, since under Doria he was eventually expelled from the Order. (Gracian died in Brussels on September 21, 1614, still following the "discalced" way of life, but within a community of brother
Carmelites of the Ancient Observance.)

Returning from Italy after his election by the Lisbon Chapter,
Doria reconvened the Chapter in October 1585 at Pastrana. He divided the province into four vicariates, each governed by a provincial vicar. John of the Cross was appointed vicar for Andalusia, while
also remaining prior of Granada. For John, the next years were of
travelling and of new foundations. In 1588, at a Chapter in Madrid,
John was elected first definitor and member of the *consulta,* Doria's
new and controversial centralized governing board for the
discalced. John was chosen prior of Segovia, seat of the *consulta,* in
the hope that he might find benefactors and oversee improvements.

In June 1591, John attended another Chapter in Madrid. According to one version of events, Fr. Doria's uneasiness about John
had been growing in recent months, partly because he suspected
John disapproved of his extreme actions against Gracián, and partly
because he mistakenly thought John was behind a recourse the nuns

had made to Rome to be free from Doria's interventions. John, realizing that many Chapter members felt intimidated from expressing their true sentiments, asked unsuccessfully for secret voting.[15]
He himself spoke out fearlessly in opposition to radical measures
against the nuns and Gracían. In the end, whether as a punishment
or not, John was left without offices, as he had wished. In fact, John
had volunteered for Mexico, a proposal unanimously accepted by
the Chapter. Yet Doria later changed his mind about John, and considered sending him back to Segovia as prior.[16]

John set off for Andalusia, thinking he was on his way to
Mexico. He stayed first at La Peñuela, where he reworked his commentary on the *Living Flame of Love*. During this time Fr. Diego
Evangelista, a revengeful, suspicious, and self-centered friar whom
John had once reprimanded, began a deplorable process of at-
tempting to disgrace John by insinuating that his interactions with
the many nuns he directed had been improper. Diego Evangelista,
now a member of Doria's *consulta*, was not prevented by the latter in
his attempted humiliation of John. This same Diego Evangelista also
helped Doria in gathering information against other opponents,
notably Gracián, who eventually admitted to some slight indiscre-
tion in his dealings with some nuns. Although not referring to any
immorality, Doria's men made it imply such. Gracián was imprisoned for months as his case was decided. Judged guilty, he was
stripped of his habit after refusing to accept his punishment, and
expelled from the order in 1592, two months after John's death. He
went to Rome for justice, but Doria made sure he got no audience.
While in Italy he was captured by Turkish pirates, taken to Tunis,
and imprisoned in an underground dungeon for two years. He was
ransomed and returned to Rome, where the pope ordered the
discalced to readmit him, but they refused. Ironically, the Car–
melites of the Ancient Observance welcomed him and allowed him
to observe the rule of the reformed.[17]

John became ill and was transferred to Ubeda for treatment.
There he was humiliated by yet another vengeful friar who still re-
sented having been corrected by John many years before: Francisco
Crisóstomo, now the prior. Informed of John's mistreatment, Fr.
Antonio, John's first companion in the reform and now provincial
of Andalusia, hastened to Ubeda to rectify the treatment of John.

John of the Cross died at midnight on Saturday, December 14, 1591. He was 49 years old, and had given himself to the reform for 23 years.[18]

The Wisdom of John of the Cross

John was under five feet tall, thin from his sacrifice and imprisonment, and oval faced with a little growth of beard and mustache. He wore the rough brown habit of the reform, a coarse white mantle, and sometimes a dark brown skull-cap. Contemporaries said that, although clearly ascetical, he had a pleasing appearance and was interesting to talk to. He was always in control of himself; peaceful, calm, and quietly joyful. He was simple, straightforward, and shunned outward manifestations of authority. Those who knew him said he was polite and delicate in dealing with others, and could share both their manual work and their recreation. He loved the beauty of nature, and deep friendships (such as that of Teresa or his brother Francisco) were important to him. He was a compassionate person, particularly sensitive to the poor, sick, and suffering. Above all, John was a giant in the spiritual life, drawing teachings of universal value from experience, both his own and others.[19]

We have glanced over John's biography, and found that his early life already showed traces of values that were to make up the general direction of his future. He could see, in the example of his parents, what it means to sacrifice all for the sake of true love. The poverty of his family showed him that mere accumulation of things does not guarantee love and happiness. However, the pain and struggles that came with the poverty made John sensitive to deprivation in others and always ready to alleviate it where he could. His family fostered piety, and John treasured such attitudes throughout his life, especially devotion to Mary. Compassionate charity, learned especially in his hospital service, became a permanent feature of his concern for others. At considerable personal sacrifice, John always integrated study into his life, from the early years in Medina de Campo right up to his last years in Andalusia. Deep love for God and others was the special quality that permeated John's whole life, as it did his message. Poverty, charity, piety, study, and deep love formed permanent parts of John's life.

John was a man of destiny. From his early life, when friends have all kinds of plans for him, he has a clear picture of what he wants from life. He has a sense of vocation—personally called by God. He works in the hospital, is successful, enjoys the work, but knows there is more to life than generous, successful ministry. He goes to the Jesuit school in Medina, thoroughly enjoys study, values it all his life, but recognizes that for him there is more to life than education. Entering the Order of Mount Carmel, attracted by its spirit of contemplation and Marian piety, he has a happy novitiate and learns to encounter God in new ways. But this experience, too, great as it is, does not satisfy John's yearning for God. He then goes to Salamanca for theology, a chance to study about God, but no amount of study alone leads him to union with God. He decides to join the Carthusians, but Teresa encourages him to seek the deeper contemplative union he wants in her renewed Carmel. By the age of 25, John has learned that ministry, education, religious life, and theology do not automatically insure union with God. Even reforming an institution to facilitate the life one seeks is no guarantee. John senses an irresistible attraction to God and pursues this goal uncompromisingly and relentlessly. What he has he values but, without despising previous experiences, he leaves them aside to continue the search in new ways.

Some people accumulate many small manifestations of love for God; others make a single-minded, single-hearted choice for love of God, and see everything as secondary to the quest for God's love. Accumulated love rarely implies renunciation; choice-oriented love always does. The seeker renounces all that up to the present was viewed as the best means available, renounces without despising previous means, moves forward to the goal of life. Choice-love is creative of one's personality, as is evident in John, who seeks God even through the nights, journeying to the union he longs for. Accumulated small expressions of love never substitute for choice-oriented love, even though they may help to manifest and maintain it. Choice-oriented love is the clearest indicator of ongoing conversion, while accumulated love can still be shown by someone who refuses to face the need for a new conversion (as we have seen in post-Vatican II times when some "renew" themselves in superficial ways without accepting the Council's call for deeper change).

John integrates all the best values from his experience in one great thrust of self-dedication to God. His goal is always clear, never neglected or watered down; he pursues it with the united effort of all his strength and talents. His is not a selfish goal of personal growth, for he takes others along with him, sharing the vision and the love by which he feels drawn.

John shows us how to live in a struggle-filled post-conciliar church, since John himself entered Carmel the year the Council of Trent concluded its deliberations. He learned to cope with people who resist the renewal he wanted, with ecclesiastical authorities interested in the power that religion brings, with the spite of some, the envy of others, and dishonest slander of still others. Through all his struggles, he maintains right priorities and proves that contemplative union is possible under any circumstances. A man of wisdom, he has journeyed to the mountaintop and can guide us too.[20]

CHAPTER TWO

The Writings of
John of the Cross

John's Ministry of the Written Word

John of the Cross was above all a mystic, who shared his knowledge of the journey to God through his spiritual direction of others. He directed people from all walks of life, lay, religious men and women, and clergy; young people, the poor, wealthy merchants, benefactors, and the nobility. Prior to his imprisonment in Toledo in 1577–1578, most of John's ministry focused on the reform, his formation of new friars, and his spiritual direction of the nuns under Teresa's care, especially during his years at the convent of the Incarnation. John spontaneously wrote poetry for his own support and consolation. His prose work came later. He apparently did not write much in his last years. So John's oral teaching and spiritual direction preceded, accompanied, and followed his written *magisterium.* John accomplished most of his writing between 1578 and 1588.

After six months in the Toledo Carmelite prison, a new warden brought John the writing material he requested, and he wrote down some of his earliest poetry, to express his inner spirit at that dreadful time. The material circumstances were hardly conducive to writing; his cell was unpleasant, damp, and had only a small loophole in the wall through which the noonday light could enter. Nevertheless, the spiritual maturing of those brutal months produced the first 31 stanzas of the "Spiritual Canticle," the "Romances," and at least two other poems.[21] John's writing shows a spiritual maturity, the result of personal experience and years of directing others, together with a good knowledge of Scripture and theology.[22]

In the year before he died some of John's writings were destroyed by nuns concerned about the nasty insinuations of Diego Evangelista. None of the original manuscripts of John's major works remains; the longest autograph is the twelve pages of the *Sayings of Light and Love*. We also have some of his original letters, and an early copy of the *Canticle* in another hand, with what may be John's handwritten corrections added, but nothing else. Fortunately, his works have come to us through numerous copies, which are more or less faithful. This raises the need for critical scholarship to determine the most accurate original reading.

There are about a thousand pages of John's work in most modern editions, which is not much when compared to other Doctors of the Church. His writings can be classified into three groups: First, his four major works are poetry and prose together—poems that he comments on stanza by stanza and verse by verse. A second group of writings are exclusively poetical, less than three hundred stanzas of verse in all; these include ten "romances" or ballads, five poetical "glosses," and two other poems. And finally we have John's shorter prose works, including the *Sayings of Light and Love, Precautions, Counsels to a Religious, Censure and Opinion,* and about thirty letters.

As mentioned already, John spontaneously wrote poetry to express his inner mystical experiences. He could then return to the poems to rekindle the original experience or to gain perspective in moments of anguish. At times, he writes because someone asks him to explain the meaning of his poetry. Thus, he explains the stanzas of the "Spiritual Canticle" because Mother Anne of Jesus, prioress of the discalced Carmelites in Granada, asked him to. Likewise the commentary on the "Living Flame of Love" was written in response to a request from Doña Ana de Peñalosa, John's friend and a benefactress of the community in Granada. Often his letters include answers to explicit requests, as does the letter of April 14, 1589, addressed to a Carmelite friar, and sent from Segovia. Sometimes, John writes in greater detail because he wants to help resolve real needs he sees. This is the case with the *Ascent of Mount Carmel,* as

John states explicitly in the Prologue (A, Prologue, 3). As we look back over four centuries of John's influence in the spiritual development of so many Christians, we can also appreciate that God inspired John to write for the benefit of the church. His writing ministry was a charism that has brought blessings to innumerable disciples throughout the centuries.

John sees his writing as a genuine expression of his own ministry. The shorter maxims clearly prolong the effectiveness of his spiritual direction, as he supports or challenges directees he has met at other times or in other places. His major works, presented as direct responses to individuals, were hardly intended to be restricted to them. John was well aware that his work would be shared with others, especially the friars and nuns of the Teresian reform. John's dedications are signs of respect to special individuals whose requests give him the occasion to speak to a wider audience. In fact, although the *Canticle* and *Living Flame* have been mentioned as addressed especially to specific individuals, their content clearly speaks to many others. All John's works manifest broad ecclesial sensitivities; they contain a universal call to holiness and prayer.

Anyone reading John today is faced with the usual problems one meets when dealing with works from another period of history. Many of John's expressions may seem unusual, even unacceptable, to contemporary readers.[23] His approach to Scripture is different,[24] his lack of an explicit liturgical focus is noticeable. His emphasis on suffering may seem exaggerated, and his seemingly negative approach to this world and its values will undoubtedly put off many. But we cannot afford to let forms of expression distract us from content. The presentation is culturally restricted in certain ways, but the basic content, the dynamic of the spiritual life, is perennially challenging.

People who want to understand John's contemporary challenge should read his work directly, frequently, and reflectively. Since many Christians have had bad initial experiences of John through misinterpretations of him, it is crucial that readers leave aside any former prejudice and be open to John's influence, enthusiasm, and challenge. His commentaries help us understand the stages or dynamics in his system of spiritual growth. Consequently, readers should not bother with digressions but keep focused on the main line of the spiritual process. Each of the major works has a different point of view, and we should try to understand each, one at a time, as we do with the four gospels. Thus the *Canticle* leads us through the journey of love, the *Ascent* through the journey of faith, each having its own rhythms. We do not read John merely to gain clearer understanding of how people understood discipleship in the sixteenth century, but to gain insight into the nature of Christian commitment and spiritual growth in our own time. So we must read John with an eye on our own situations—personal, ecclesial, and societal.[25] The poems are the most faithful and life-giving expression of John's thought, and so, once we have a good understanding of his doctrine, as presented particularly in his commentaries, we can return frequently to the poems, letting them speak to us with constant freshness. The poems do a work of formation whether or not we read the prose.

The Greatest Poet of the Spanish Language

John was an artist. We know he sketched well, since we have the picture of the crucifixion he drew. He carved and sculpted, and his work was used in the new foundations. He also designed two of the monasteries, built under his direction; the cloister in Segovia and the aqueduct in Granada are still admired. He was not embarrassed to express himself in dance, song, and drama. However, John expressed his inner feelings most naturally in poetry. Both Menéndez Pelayo and Dámaso Alonso claim that John is the greatest poet of the Spanish language.[26]

We do not know if John had read much poetry apart from his classes in the humanities at Medina, although religious communities used poetry at times in their services, and individuals held competitions in writing poems on a religious theme.[27] One form of poetry that influenced John is the *villancico*, which begins with a theme stated in two to three lines, the last of which is then repeated at the end of each stanza. John's poem, "For I know well the spring," is in precisely this popular form, each stanza echoing the last line of the initial theme-verse, "Although it is night." Religious in John's day often took popular love songs and reworked them, modifying them slightly so that they expressed love between themselves and Christ. This transposition of a secular song to a religious level is seen in those poems that are introduced with the words *a lo divino* [with a spiritual meaning]. One of John's most beautiful poems, "A lone young shepherd," is of this kind. John's ten romances follow the usual ballad meter and verse form of the time. These poetical narratives maintain the same rhyme throughout by ending alternate lines with the same sound—generally a verb in the Spanish imperfect or conditional tense.

John's three major poems, the "Spiritual Canticle," the "Dark Night", and the "Living Flame," show the influence of three Spanish poets. Garcilasco de la Vega, who died six years before John's birth, introduced the Italian Renaissance style of poetry to Spain. One of his innovations was to extend the Spanish meter by three syllables. John used this hendecasyllabic meter in his great poems. Garcilasco was influenced by his friend Juan Boscán, and their poetry was published in one volume by Boscan's widow in 1543, a year after her husband's death. John may well have read their work when studying in Medina del Campo. In 1575, while John was in Avila, an Andalusian, Sebastián de Córdoba published a collection of religious adaptations of Garcilasco's poetry, and since John quotes from it, we know he read it. Garcilasco further influenced John by emphasizing pastoral themes in his work, as John does in the "Spiritual Canticle."[28]

Mystics frequently use the imagery and symbolism of the biblical Song of Songs (or Canticle of Canticles), portraying various scenes in a growing relationship of two lovers, leading up to their union in marriage. John's "Canticle" takes its title from this book of Hebrew Scripture, and both the "Canticle" and the poem of the "Dark Night" follow the model of the lovers' yearnings in the Song of Songs.

Leaving the major works for later consideration, let us briefly examine the themes of the minor poetical works. The "Romances" are an important part of John's theological vision. While the four major prose works portray the disciple's journey to God, the "Romances" synthesize John's understanding of salvation history. Focusing on God's plan for the world, they complement the seeker's return journey to God. The nine interlinked "Romances" "on the

Gospel text 'In principio erat Verbum' " present poetical reflections
on the Trinity and the Incarnation. Important for their doctrinal
synthesis, their simple and beautifully expressed doctrines are rich
in their biblical, trinitarian, christological, and ecclesiological understanding and vision. The first portrays the inner life of the Most
Holy Trinity in its eternal, atemporal, mutual loving. This vision of
God is also foundational for the disciple's return journey to God.

> As the lover in the beloved
> each lived in the other,
> and the Love that unites them
> is one with them,
>
> . . . .
> Thus it is a boundless
> Love that unites them,
> for the three have one love
> which is their essence;
> and the more love is one
> the more it is love.

The second "Romance" deals with the internal communication among the Persons of the Trinity. It is a communication in love
already heralded as the basis for the Father's love of the Son's future disciples.

> In that immense love
> proceeding from the two
> the Father spoke words
> of great affection to the Son,
>
> . . . .
> "...and whoever is like you in nothing
> will find nothing in me.
> I am pleased with you alone
> O life of my life!"

The third to sixth "Romances" speak about creation. The third
is a dialogue between Father and Son, the former wanting a bride
for the Son, the latter wanting a bride who glorifies the Father. Thus
creation becomes a project of love between the Father and the Son,
the palace in which the spouse will dwell. The body of the spouse is

constituted of all the just. Although endowed with a lower nature, humankind will be specially blessed when the Son becomes human too. The promise of the fourth "Romance" becomes the hope of the fifth, a hope portrayed in terms of Israel's longings. This hope culminates in Simeon's recognition of the light that descended from the heights (sixth "Romance"). The seventh "Romance" proclaims the Incarnation in which the lover will become:

> "Like the one he loves;
> for the greater their likeness
> the greater their delight."
>
> . . . .
> "I will go seek my bride
> and take upon myself
> her weariness and labors
> in which she suffers so;
> and that she may have life
> I will die for her,
> and, lifting her out of that deep,
> I will restore her to you."

The eighth and ninth "Romances" bring the hope, the plan, and the promise into history through the revelation of the conception and birth through the Mother, Mary. Thus, the Son comes to his bride, the church:

> embracing his bride,
> holding her in his arms,
> whom the gracious Mother
> laid in a manger....

A tenth "Romance" based on psalm 137, "By the Waters of Babylon," portrays the psalmist's pain, hope, and longing for deliverance, for salvation brought in Jesus. It culminates in verse 14:

> ...and he will gather his little ones
> And me, who wept because of you,
> at the rock who is Christ
> for whom I abandoned you.

John also wrote five poetic "glosses," that is, series of stanzas that comment on a basic theme, repeating it in the last line of each stanza. "I entered into unknowing," described as "stanzas concerning an ecstasy experienced in high contemplation," actually reads more like a commentary on the *Ascent* and "Dark Night". Imagery decreases, and the gloss ends by explaining the concept of unknowing. Every stanza ends by affirming that it is an unknowing "transcending all knowledge."

"I live, but not in myself" comments on the intense suffering of one who longs to see God.[29] The seeker can say:

> I do not desire this life
> *I am dying because I do not die.*
>
> . . . .
> I will cry out for death
>
> . . . .
> O my God, when will it be
> That I can truly say:
> *Now I live because I do not die?*

Thus the seeker in death finds the life, always longed for.

"I went out seeking love" is a gloss that substitutes the image of hunting for prey instead of longing for love. It is a secular poem to which John gives a religious interpretation of hope.

"Without support yet with support" is a short poem to which John gives a religious interpretation; the disciple, dissatisfied with every created thing, longs for the love of God. The three stanzas successively focus on faith, hope, and charity.

"Not for all of beauty" is a secular poem that takes on extraordinary meaning for John, who (as we will later see) identifies beauty as the essence of God. Once a disciple has tasted the beauty of God, nothing else will ever bring satisfaction.

In addition to the "Romances", the glosses, and the poems on which his major prose works are based, John wrote two further poems of exceptional beauty. "For I know well the spring" describes how a disciple "rejoices in knowing God through faith." The result of John's extraordinary mystical experiences in the Toledo prison, this poem was probably written on the octave of the feast of Corpus Christi. Deprived for six months of either celebrating the Eucharist or receiving communion, surrounded by the darkness of his prison cell, John professes his own knowledge of God through faith. John gives the poem an exceptional doctrinal development from the eternal uncreated divinity, to belief in the Trinity, Incarnation, and the presence of the Lord in the Eucharist that we receive in communion. The poem has a simple rhythm that remind us of a flowing river—an image that John uses for the life of grace. John's prison on the banks of the Tagus would have suggested both the night and the river that are the principle symbols in this poem. "A lone young shepherd" (the *Pastorcico*) is a beautiful love poem that John uses to express the love between Christ and the disciple. By changing only the last verse, John gives a new meaning to the whole poem which now culminates in the loving surrender of Christ on the cross.

John's Shorter Prose Works

John of the Cross, always a person of many responsibilities, gave primary importance to his ministry of spiritual direction. He maintained his directive and supportive contacts with many directees through letters or short spiritual maxims, both manifesting John's solid spiritual teaching.

The *Sayings of Light and Love,* a collection of seventy some short sayings, are particularly important because the original manuscript is preserved (in the parish church of Andújar, in the province of Jaén). The original is damaged at the beginning and end, leading some commentators to suggest there may have been more sayings in the collection. The numbering of the sayings, added later, varies slightly according to editions and translations.

From the time he was chaplain at the Incarnation, John established the practice of distributing to his directees and penitents small cards with a spiritual maxim to focus their commitment.[30] Later, when provincial vicar in Andalusia, and unable to give as much time as he wanted to the nuns of the Teresian reform, he would leave each of them some short written advice. These spiritual sayings were often passed from one religious to another. Gradually, individuals or communities made collections of John's sayings, even extracting key maxims from his major works. Given the variety of collections, and the possibility of modifications and additions, the authenticity of the sayings is difficult to determine. Hence the particular importance of the Andújar collection, whose authenticity is evident.[31] These sayings are an excellent example of how John applied his system to individuals.

The structure of the sayings is very simple but not monotonous, as is frequently the case with this sort of collection. Some are quite poetical (Sayings, 16), and others are extraordinary in successfully condensing John's spiritual vision in a single statement (15). Some are maxims for life (60), advice in confronting dangers (66), prayers (50), or confessions (39).

The major themes of the sayings are the necessity of spiritual direction, denial of one's appetites, the importance of being guided by reason rather than feeling or taste, the nature of authentic love, and intimacy with God.

One of the sayings included in the original, sometimes left unnumbered in modern versions, or listed as 26, is the "Prayer of a Soul Taken with Love." Of particular literary, theological, and mystical value, this saying develops in a continuing crescendo from the misery of sin, to humble abandonment, to confidence in Jesus, and finally to the enthusiastic possession of everything in the Lord.

> ...Mine are the heavens and mine is the earth. Mine are the nations, the just are mine, and mine the sinners. The angels are mine, and the Mother of God, and all things are mine; and God himself is mine and for me, because Christ is mine and all for me.

In addition to the Andújar collection of *Sayings of Light and Love,* there are other similar collections: *Maxims on Love,* the *Degrees of Perfection,* and *Other Counsels.* Some editions also add the nine *Counsels of Madre Magdalena,* maxims very similar to those given in chapter 13 of the first book of the *Ascent.*

It is generally suggested that John wrote the *Precautions* for the nuns in Beas, during 1578–1579, while he was their confessor. Some commentators, impressed by the fact that the masculine gender is used throughout, consider they may have been recopied and adapted for the friars' community of El Calvario, when John was prior in 1578–79. The *Precautions* are a group of nine norms to keep in mind in order to avoid typical dangers in religious life. The nine warnings are in three groups of three, directed against the classical enemies of the spiritual life: world, devil, and flesh. There is a dynamic development from external dangers to difficulties within oneself. Each precaution has a similar structure: a warning, advantages from observing the warning, harm from its omission. Against threats from the world John advises detachment; against threats from the devil he recommends that religious do nothing outside of obedience; against threats from the weakness of flesh he urges that we seek that which is least desirable.

The first warning against the world has caused much discussion, since John says to religious: "Withdraw your heart from relatives as much as from others, and in some ways even more." This warning is not directed against the values of family life and love, but rather is against tribalism and the false pride in lineage and social status that family or "blood" can bring. This was a serious difficulty in sixteenth century Spain, as we already saw when the family of John's father rejected him because he married a poor woman, outside the family's social class.

The three warnings against the devil recommend overcoming his assaults by obedience, while the precautions against weaknesses of the flesh advocate always choosing the more difficult. To some readers this may sound masochistic, and they may feel that John's obedience would be irresponsible passivity today. However, a careful reading of his advice shows that John is simply recommending detachment from one's own agenda and selfish interests. We must learn to find our pleasure in God's will. We must learn to focus attention on what is primary in our lives—the search for God—and let the secondary issues take care of themselves.

The *Precautions* contain a lot of practical wisdom and have applications beyond the confines of religious life. Moreover, they can be means for the passive purification of spirit.

Similar in both style and content to the *Precautions* are the *Counsels to a Religious on How to Reach Perfection,* addressed probably to a lay brother or a student. The four counsels are resignation, mortification, practice of virtue, and solitude. The first counsel corresponds to the third precaution against the world; the second to the first precaution against the flesh; the third to the second and third precautions against the flesh; and the fourth to the first precaution against the devil.

Depending on how they are numbered, we have some 32 or 33 *Letters* of John of the Cross. Of these we have eleven in John's original handwriting, and copies of three other originals. They all belong to the last ten years of John's life, 1581–1591. Three of the letters are official (10, 14, 18), one is a narrative, and the rest deal with spiritual direction. Unfortunately, many of John's letters were destroyed by recipients during the final persecution. Yet although we have none to his family, or to Teresa of Avila, some offer auto-biographical material regarding John's role in foundations (5, 21), his feelings and interests (11, 12), and his own state of mind and heart during his final persecution (25).

Sometimes included in collections of John's letters is the "Censure and Opinion" on a discalced Carmelite nun's prayer life. Requested by Fr. Doria to examine the nun, John identifies five weaknesses in her approach to prayer. This response was probably written from Segovia sometime in 1588–1591.

John's correspondence gives us insight into concrete applications of his teachings to individuals he knew and loved. Some themes are frequent: the night, the spirit of poverty, the love of God, silence, and solitude.

John's Four Major Prose Works

John's four major works are the *Ascent of Mount Carmel*, the *Dark Night*, the *Spiritual Canticle*, and the *Living Flame of Love*. All four deal with aspects of the whole journey to God. The first two use the image of the night and describe especially the journey of faith, whereas the *Canticle* and *Living Flame* use matrimonial or nuptial imagery and stress the journey of love.[32]

The Ascent of Mount Carmel

John wrote this treatise between 1581 and 1585, beginning it while he was in the Andalusian monastery of El Calvario, continuing it while he was rector in Baeza, and completing it while he was prior in Granada. We possess the reliable handwritten copy of Fr. Juan Evangelista, John's secretary and confessor.

In effect, though each has a distinct title, the *Ascent* and the *Dark Night* together form one work, which must be understood as a unity in life and doctrine.[33] Generally, they are placed first among the prose commentaries in the editions of John's writings, because they are most detailed regarding the earlier stages of the spiritual life. Nevertheless, their teaching is very difficult both to understand and to accept, and most readers should probably be introduced to some of John's other works before these.

Each of John's major prose works is preceded by its corresponding poem, which, in most cases, he explains line by line.[34] The poem thus becomes a means to focus the reader's attention. The *Ascent* is preceded by the same poem as the *Dark Night,* and the latter in particular provides a commentary on its initial stanzas. The pedagogical aid that John uses for the *Ascent* is not so much the poem as the diagram or sketch of Mount Camel. John considered this diagram an important visual synthesis of his doctrine in the treatise, and he made many copies for the nuns in Beas and friars in Baeza and Granada. Moreover, he explicitly refers to its placement at the beginning of his treatise (A, 1, 13, 10). The diagram shows Mount Carmel—"Only the honor and glory of God dwells on this mountain." On the peak of the mountain John indicates the abundant rewards awaiting those who arrive at the peak: the fruits and gifts of the Holy Spirit. Those who seek to arrive at the mountaintop of union with God can choose one of three ways to the summit. Two of them are broad roads, to the left and right: "ways of the imperfect spirit," consisting in the pursuit of the "goods of heaven" or "the goods of earth." Seekers who follow these broad roads become attached to the heavenly or earthly goods that are merely a means to God. In the center of the diagram is the narrow "path of the perfect spirit" on which John has written *nada* [nothing] seven times. Only the middle way leads to divine union.[35]

When John describes this center path in the treatise, there are a few lines that suggest ascent, others that suggest a plateau, and still others that suggest descent. Although it eventually leads to the mountain top, this rough, narrow path presents the climber with many ups and downs. Lest we do injustice to John by stressing his seven "nothings"—he has been called Doctor of the *nadas*—it is more correct to say that the radical attitude necessary in ascending the middle path up the mountain is "all-nothing" (*todo y nada*), since the climber is dedicated to attaining the *fullness* of life to which the sacrifices of the climb lead. This radical attitude is explained at the bottom of the diagram where the three spiritual powers—will (tasting or receiving satisfaction), intellect (knowing), and memory (possessing)—are redirected by the three theological virtues: charity, faith, and hope, respectively.

The *Ascent* is the fruit of long experience and personal observation. It is a serious treatise with a logical structure, mental rigor, and solid biblical foundations—all important themes are introduced with Scripture (A, 1, 5; 2, 7; 2, 22; 3, 16). John acknowledges that the subject matter is difficult, but he feels compelled to deal with it because "it is extremely necessary to so many souls" (A, Prologue, 3) whom God calls to union, but whose spiritual directors do not understand the dynamic of spiritual growth. In the *Ascent* John deals especially (though not exclusively) with the active nights.

The principle divisions of the work are: Book One, a general introduction to the active night of sense and the mortification of the appetites; Book Two, a general introduction to the active night of spirit and its expressions in the active night of the intellect in faith; and Book Three, on the active night of the spirit as it purifies the memory in hope and the will in charity.

The scheme of the *Ascent* directs our attention to the three theological virtues, which become the focus of the work of purification and rectification of our "dis-integrated" human nature.

Although the *Ascent* is a masterpiece, it is important to concentrate on the content, the dynamic process, and not on the scholastic or negative-sounding language that some may find distracting. The reader must distinguish between what is said, and how it is said.

The Dark Night

John escaped from the prison in Toledo in August 1578, and after the Almodóvar chapter was sent to El Calvario, where he stayed for about eight months, before founding Baeza in June. During those months at El Calvario, it seems, when he was also confessor at

Beas, John wrote the poem, "Noche oscura" [Dark Night], while his own experience of the night in Toledo was still fresh in his memory. John probably began the commentary while in Baeza, before the *Ascent* was complete, then worked on both, finishing both in Granada (1584–85).

The poem that precedes the commentary is the living expression of his spiritual experience. Its images of night and flight differ from the active climbing and effort of the *Ascent*. Although referring to the purifying darkness experienced in spiritual growth, the poem is written after the pain and suffering have passed, with the perspective and awareness that the Lord was leading through the night to loving union. Hence, the "dark night" is also "that glad night," "guiding night," "night more lovely than the dawn," and "night that has united the Lover with his beloved."

The *Ascent* and the *Dark Night* are complementary, forming a diptych, two parts of the one journey to God. The *Ascent* deals primarily with the active nights of sense and spirit, while the *Dark Night* deals with the passive nights of sense and spirit. These are not two distinct paths between which seekers can choose, but two aspects of one unique active-passive journey to God. In fact, the Prologue to the *Dark Night* speaks of the same path leading to the summit of Mount Carmel, and adds "this narrow road is called a dark night."

John sees the *Dark Night* commentary as strictly united with the *Ascent*, treating the former as Book Four of the *Ascent*, and frequently giving reference in one to the other, as if they were both parts of the same treatise. In the *Living Flame* he refers to *"the Dark Night of the Ascent of Mount Carmel"* (F, 1, 25).

In this second work, complementary to the *Ascent*, John once again repeats the entire "Dark Night" poem, and starts to comment on it a second time, from a new perspective. In fact, he actually only comments on stanzas 1 and 2, presents the third, and then ends abruptly, perhaps because he believes he has already achieved his purpose of explaining the nature of the passive nights. Book One deals with the passive night of sense, and Book Two deals with the passive night of spirit. In both cases the passive purification is achieved through contemplation.

There are more copies of the *Dark Night* commentary than of any other of John's works, but none of them claim to be a transcript of the original. Textual critics consider that the two most trustworthy codices are those in the National Library of Madrid and in the general archives of Discalced Carmelite Friars in Rome.

The Spiritual Canticle

This text begins and ends John's work as a writer. He wrote the first 31 verses of the poem when in prison in Toledo (1577–78), and additional verses while prior in Granada (1582–84). As far as we can now tell, he wrote the commentary bit by bit in Granada in 1584, touching it up for two more years, producing the definitive text in Los Mártires, Granada, in 1586. John worked with more care on the *Canticle* than on any other work, giving it almost eight years of his life.

The title is not John's, but that of his first disciples and biographers. It does, however, reflect John's own approach. The poem follows the imagery of the biblical Song of Songs. John calls the poem "songs (*canciones*) between the soul and her spouse," and presents the commentary as "a declaration of the songs." The *Canticle* describes the progressive acquisition of divine love. The symbolism is nuptial, and the tone almost exclusively affective.

There are two versions of the *Canticle* poem and commentary, both authentic, the second not supplanting the first but making different choices.[36] The first redaction follows the logic of love; the structure of the second is more pedagogical. As John continued to touch up the work, he gave various interpretations to the poem, and thus the two principle versions emerged. The first (A) has 39 stanzas; the commentary is shorter, the quotations are in Latin, and the last five stanzas seem to speak of an earthly perfection attained through mystical marriage. Both the poem and the commentary are more spontaneous and lyrical. The second edition (B) has 40 stanzas; John added stanza 11 and changed the order of the 18 intermediate stanzas (16–33 in B). The commentary is longer and more logical; he adds an introduction at the beginning of most sections, and annotations before each stanza. The last five stanzas are more clearly related to eternal life, of which mystical marriage provides only the foretaste. This second version is doctrinally more valuable and manifests greater clarity and order. The B redaction of the *Canticle* commentary refers to the *Living Flame* (31, 7), and thus was written after the composition of the *Flame* in 1585–86.

All codices of the *Canticle* indicate that it was written, at least in its initial version, at the request of Ann of Jesus (Ana de Jesús), prioress of the discalced Carmelite nuns of St. Joseph's in Granada.

The *Canticle* commentary is not divided into chapters or books, but simply follows the stanzas of the poem. John explains the four major divisions in stanza 22 of the B redaction (C, 22, 3): 1) an anxious search for one loved (st. 1–12); 2) the joy and preoccupation of the encounter with the loved one—spiritual espousal (st. 13–21); 3) the total union, insofar as is possible in this life, and resulting fruits—spiritual marriage (st. 22–35); 4) desire and glory (st. 36–40). John modifies the rhythm of the poem to adapt to its content. Thus, stanzas 1–12, which describe the anxious search, contain no adjectives or adverbs in Spanish, but portray quick movement with no concern for details, only the longing to find one's lover as quickly as possible. These stanzas contrast with stanzas 13–21, which contain numerous adjectives and convey the broad, expressive fullness and satisfaction of encounter.

The *Canticle* poem was born in the prison of Toledo, from John's own mystical experiences that he struggled to express in poetry, jotting down 31 stanzas in a notebook that Madre Magdalena del Espíritu Santo testified she saw after his escape. The stanzas "were obviously composed with a certain burning love of God." However, John warns us, "it would be foolish to think that expressions of love arising from mystical understanding, like these stanzas, are fully explainable" (C, Prologue, 1). John goes on to ask:

> Who can describe in writing the understanding he gives to loving souls in whom he dwells? And who can express with words the experience he imparts to them? Who, finally, can explain the desires he gives them? Certainly, no one can! Not even they who receive these communications. (Ibid.)

John urges readers to approach the text with simplicity of spirit. "It is better to explain the utterances of love in their broadest sense so that each one may derive profit from them according to the mode and capacity of one's own spirit" (C, Prologue, 2). Although broadly autobiographical, following his own search for loving union with the divine, the *Canticle* speaks to all who long for life with God.[37]

The Living Flame of Love

Both the poem and the commentary were written for Doña Ana de Peñalosa. Fr. Juan Evangelista claimed that John wrote the *Living Flame* commentary in fifteen days when he was living in Granada as vicar provincial for Andalusia.[38] Since John held this office from October, 1585 to April, 1587, we have an approximate time frame for the composition of the original commentary. John later revised it while at La Peñuela, between August and September of 1591, thus giving us redaction B of the *Living Flame* commentary, slightly different from the first version. It is interesting that John could write about the last stage of love precisely when he was the object of a systematic humiliation by the bitter Diego Evangelista.

The title is taken from the first verse of the poem. The poem consists of four stanzas of six lines each, a poetic format original with John. He uses the longer stanzas to achieve the scope of his work. They are slower and richer, giving the impression of fullness and satisfaction. Where one would expect the stanzas to end (after line four), they go on for another two lines. Thus, he creates the dynamism of the abundant satisfaction of love.

Although focused on the present joy of union with God, each of the first three verses has a retrospective line, as present joy reminds the seeker of previous suffering that led to this union. The last stanza, focused entirely on the present, is permeated with peace.

The commentary follows the order of the four stanzas, seen as four facets of the same state of spiritual marriage. John uses the opportunity of the three retrospective lines to make long digressions on previous stages, especially the passive nights. The digressions, which comprise a third of the work, make this useful reading even for individuals who have not reached the state of transformation.

Unlike John's other works, this one is not progressive, through a series of spiritual stages. "Even though it is true that what these and the other stanzas describe is all one state of transformation, and as such one cannot pass beyond it; yet, with time and practice, love can grow deeper in quality, as I say, and become more ardent" (F, Prologue, 3). According to the commentary, stanza one describes the individual's life when inflamed by the Holy Spirit. Stanza two describes the life-giving work of the Trinity in the individual. The third stanza shows that the attributes of the Trinity are revealed vitally (i.e. each Person reveals particular attributes by loving the soul with the force of that attribute). Finally, stanza four presents the individual communing with the Word and experiencing the whole created cosmos in God.

The poem uses the symbolism of flame and fire that burn, purify, and transform wood placed on the fire. "This flame of love is the Spirit of the Bridegroom, who is the Holy Spirit" (F, 1, 3). Gradually, the log of wood becomes one with the fire, as the individual is drawn into union with God through the work of the Holy Trinity. "The three Persons of the Most Blessed Trinity, the Father, the Son, and the Holy Spirit, are the ones who effect in it this divine work of union" (F, 2, 1). As the fire gives light and heat to the wood placed in it, likewise the individual receives the qualities of God (F, 3, 2). The final stage is union in "the delicate love of God," who "breathes the Holy Spirit" in the individual's heart, "absorbing it most profoundly in the Holy Spirit, rousing its love with a divine exquisite quality and delicacy" (F, 4, 17). Thus, the Holy Spirit "filled the soul with good and glory in which he enkindled it in love of himself, indescribably and incomprehensibly, in the depths of God, to whom be honor and glory forever and ever. Amen" (F, 4, 17).

John's Mystical Language

John of the Cross was a very good theologian, highly respected as a teacher and spiritual master in his own day. He understood well both church doctrine and the speculative theology of the sixteenth century's authorities. He used scholastic theology in his work (C, Prologue, 3), but above all was steeped in Scripture. His was not a historical-critical approach to the Bible, as we have today, but he had so thoroughly absorbed the biblical messages, and quotes so many books of Scripture so often, that his works have been described as a kind of "Spanish Vulgate."[39] All these sources and authorities help in expressing the realities of faith, but for the mystic they are inadequate. "The saintly doctors, no matter how much they have said or will say, can never furnish an exhaustive explanation of these figures and comparisons, since the abundant meanings of the Holy Spirit cannot be caught in words. Thus, the explanation of these expressions usually contains less than what they embody in themselves" (C, Prologue, 1).

Conceptual and speculative language may help to clarify and articulate our faith, but its vital core—our loving relationship with God—is more truly shared "in mystical theology, which is known through love and by which these truths are not only known but at the same time enjoyed" (C, Prologue, 3).[40] Profound religious experiences cannot be expressed to others in precise language. Moreover, mystical wisdom leads people to love God without fully understanding the divine life. "For mystical wisdom, which comes through love…, need not be understood distinctly in order to cause love and affection in the soul, for it is given according to the mode of faith through which we love God without understanding him" (C, Prologue, 2). Mystics, unable to express their experiences in precise language, choose figurative expressions rather than rational explanations. "These persons let something of their experience overflow in figures, comparisons, and similitudes, and from the abundance of their spirit pour out secrets and mysteries rather than rational explanations" (C, Prologue, 1).

John's major works begin with figurative titles—ascent, dark night, canticle of love, living flame—titles that already evoke responses in the hearts of believers. John then presents his poems as glimpses into his profound experiences: "unable to express the fullness of his meaning in ordinary words, [he] utters mysteries in strange figures and likenesses" (C, Prologue, 1). When disciples ask John to explain these poems he begins each one with a prologue in which he states that it is not possible to explain adequately the experiences to which the poems refer.

> The darkness and trials, spiritual and temporal, that fortu-
> nate souls ordinarily undergo on their way to the high state of

perfection are so numerous and profound that human science cannot understand them adequately. Nor does experience of them equip one to explain them. Only those who suffer them will know what this experience is like, but they won't be able to describe it. (A, Prologue, 1)

Since these stanzas, then, were composed in a love flowing from abundant mystical understanding, I cannot explain them adequately.... (C, Prologue, 2)

I have felt somewhat reluctant...to explain these four stanzas.... Since they deal with matters so interior and spiritual, for which words are usually lacking...I find it difficult to say something of their content.... (F, Prologue, 1)

John's commentaries are very clear expositions of profound religious experiences, but they also contain much imagery and symbolism; his language is often allusive rather than descriptive, and in places he even becomes carried away at the remembrance of previous experiences.

Let us so act that by means of this loving activity we may attain to the vision of ourselves in your beauty in eternal life. That is: That I be so transformed in your beauty that we may be alike in beauty, and both behold ourselves in your beauty, possessing then your very beauty; this, in such a way that each looking at the other may see in the other their own beauty, since both are your beauty alone, I being absorbed in your beauty; hence, I shall see you in your beauty, and you will see me in your beauty, and I shall see myself in you in your beauty, and you will see yourself in me in your beauty; that I may resemble you in your beauty, and you resemble me in your beauty, and my beauty be your beauty and your beauty my beauty; wherefore I shall be you in your beauty, and you will be me in your beauty, because your very beauty will be my beauty; and thus we shall behold each other in your beauty. (C, 36, 5)

Mystics, then, often choose poetry as a natural form to express the mystery of God.[41] Finding the experience ineffable, indescribable, mystics use the transformative and transcendent language of poetry—synthetic, global, creative, and always open to new meanings at other times.[42] Where poetry is not possible, mystics often use suggestive language. Thus, a mystic's expressed willingness to die a thousand deaths to have the same experience of God suggests the wonderful joy of the experience (C, 9, 2–3). In addition to poetry and hyperbole, mystics use symbols—images that bring together a set of characteristics and evoke a precise response (e.g., fire, light, night, or matrimony). For symbols to work effectively, we must both savor the reality referred to and be able to rise from it to God. Thus the image of fire should evoke an appreciation of the warmth, light, purifying, transforming, and consuming qualities of God. If the symbol of matrimony leads only to thoughts of conjugal union rather than union with God, it fails as a means of mystical expression. John's favorite symbols are those of nature (C, 4–5), matrimony (C, 22, 3), and night (A, 1, 2, 1). However, all of these forms of expressing the mystical experience require ascetical commitment on the part of the reader in order to understand and appreciate them (A, 3, 26, 5; C, 27, 1).

The Mystical Doctor shares with us part of his encounter with God and hopes thereby to fill us with equal enthusiasm and desire.[43] However, as we read John, we must remember that "these words are spirit and life. These words are perceived by souls who have ears to hear them, those souls, as I say that are cleansed and enamored" (F, 1, 5). As we approach his work, we must do so without prejudice, open to God's call. John's doctrine, his *magisterium,* is of universal value, but perhaps not all are ready to hear (F, 1, 6). Both John's life and his writings form a profound prophetic challenge for disciples of all times.

CHAPTER THREE

John's Vision of the Spiritual Life

The Nature of the Spiritual Life in John

John of the Cross's life, as well as his teachings, give the impression of a person with a unified vision in which all aspects of the human personality are well integrated. The unfortunate distinctions often made between spiritual and material life, interior and exterior life, supernatural and natural life, would find no support in John's synthesis. John calls us to integrate every dimension of human existence in one great thrust of self-dedication to the Lord.

We saw in the overview of John's life that he never stops seeking union with God. Rarely does he talk about "mystical experiences," since such experiences can be quite subjective. Rather, wishing to emphasize that the encounter with God is real, and not merely subjective, John talks about seeking union. He has a singleminded commitment to reach this union. "The soul, enamored of the Word, her Bridegroom, the Son of God, longs for union with him through clear and essential vision. She records her longings of love and complains to him of his absence" (C, 1, 2). The seeker who keeps the goal of union always in clear sight is thereby able to accept the hardships of the search. "By finding his satisfaction and strength in this love, [one] will have the courage and constancy to readily deny all other appetites" (A, 1, 14, 2).

The spiritual life is an unwavering search for a union in which seekers not only find God but also their true selves, a search that all are invited to undertake. "God gives many souls the talent and grace for advancing, and should they desire to make the effort they would arrive at this high state" (A, Prologue, 3). Although most of John's works were written for discalced Carmelites (see A, Prologue, 9), he shows great concern for laity, hardly suggesting that his ideas need to be watered down for their sakes! In fact, the work that describes the final stage of union is written expressly for a laywoman, Doña Ana de Peñalosa. Moreover, religious life in John's day was similar in many ways to that of some contemporary laity dedicated to a deeper life of prayer. His works and message apply to everyone.

John sees the spiritual life as this universal call to search constantly for union with God. It is a personal exodus from our own captivity to the promised land. All of John's major poems suggest this exodus, or departure, in their first stanzas: "One dark night, ...I went out unseen." "I went out calling you, and you were gone." "O living flame of love, ...tear through the veil of this sweet encounter." This journey to God begins after a person "has been resolutely converted to his service" (N, 1, 1, 2). Once started, "the attainment of our goal demands that we never stop on this road" (A, 1, 11, 6).

John understands the spiritual life as a continual process of growth or regression, but never stationary. He does not speak of static states of life, but rather of appetites, desires—those qualities of a person (whether good or bad), that are dynamic, constantly drawing us onward. John considers that growth must involve an integrated development, not a dissipated pursuit of several goals at once. "People are indeed ignorant who think it is possible to reach this high state of union with God without first emptying their appetite of all the natural and supernatural things that can be a hindrance to them" (A, 1, 5, 2). If each disordered appetite or desire pursues its own goal, human effort is divided and weakened. "The appetites weaken a person's virtue because they are like shoots burgeoning about a tree, sapping its strength, and causing it to be fruitless" (A, 1, 10, 2). The exodus and resulting journey is a major undertaking of love, and disciples (like John) must never relent but constantly strive to develop their positive capacities and energies, and rectify maladjusted ones. "Everyone knows that not to go forward on this road is to turn back" (A, 1, 11, 5).

This exodus of spiritual dedication is a departure from security, and implies a willingness to journey through the nights. Some disciples, rather than accept the sacrifices of this journey to God, "look for progress in what brings no progress but instead hinders them." Such individuals "work and tire themselves greatly, and yet go backwards." "It is sad to see them" (A, Prologue, 7), says John. This dark journey requires great patience and constancy in all the tribulations and trials God allows. In the second chapter of Book One of the *Ascent,* John offers three reasons why this journey can be called a night. First, the point of departure—purification of the appetites and desires—implies deprivation or loss. "This denial and privation is like a night for all one's senses." The second reason has to do with the darkness of the road travelled: "Now this road is faith, and for the intellect faith is also like a dark night." The third reason John offers "pertains to the point of arrival, namely, God," for "God is also a dark night to the soul in this life" (A, 1, 2, 1). All who long for union with God must courageously enter this threefold darkness of the journey (A, 1, 4).

Disciples who search for God through the darkness will be rewarded, and will then look back upon "that glad night," knowing that the love they had for the Lord guided their search:

> More surely than the light of noon
> to where he was awaiting me
> —him I knew so well—

Former hard times become a guiding night for individuals who receive "the sovereign favor God granted...in the intimacy of his love, which is the union with God, or transformation, through love" (C, 26, 2). Of this transforming love John says, "The soul now feels that it is all inflamed in the divine union.... It seems, because it is so forcefully transformed in God, so sublimely possessed by him, and arrayed with such rich gifts and virtues, that it is singularly close to beatitude" (F, 1, 1).

The spiritual life implies a firm, unrelenting, and enthusiastic search for union with God, what John calls a "better love," that is, a desire for Christ that is greater than all other desires (A, 1, 14, 2).

This search passes through the nights, and is, in fact, itself a night. The disciple, constantly renewing a choice-oriented love for God, makes this personal exodus and passover to a life of union. The end of the search is a transforming experience of union with God and of personal renewal.

The System Underlying John's Vision

In looking both at the history of sixteenth century Spain and at John's own life, it becomes clear that John achieved his own goal of union with God amid enormous pressures from civil and ecclesiastical authorities. When so many others were swallowed up in ecclesiastical politics, John maintains a view of religion as a movement of the Spirit. He identifies the Christian and human roots of religious experience, clarifies the source of life, and gives lots of practical advice on ways to search for and obtain this life.

Everyone lives out of an implicit system, whether they can articulate it or not. Sometimes someone else needs to synthesize the system, as happened with Teresa of Avila. An excellent systematic theologian as well as a mystic, John is able to formulate the system that underlies his thought. Analyzing his approach after four hundred years may give us the impression that it is complicated, but the opposite is true. By no means restricted to a religious elite, John's is a vital system that has its source and end in faith and love.[44] He expands his system, incorporating elements of theology, philosophy, psychology, and Scripture, but this is to support and document his views. The system presupposed in all John's works is itself simple, fruitful, relatively easy for directors to use, and available to almost everyone. We have seen that John's major works begin with a vital movement that initiates the progressive journey to God. John already has the whole journey in mind, since he has reached his destination of union with God and can look back over the terrain (N, 1, Prologue). In his commentaries, or when offering spiritual direction through his letters, maxims, or precautions, John locates his advice within the context of the systematic development of the spiritual life. So he can say to Madre Ana de San Alberto, "Prepare yourself, for God desires to grant you a great favor" (Letter 3). Praising a friar who desires passivity of the will, John can give specific directions on its attainment and can clarify what lies beyond (Letter 13). His maxims present wise intuitions into the spiritual life in view of its goal (Sayings 19, 23, 25). Moreover, John's "Censure and Opinion" of the inauthenticity of a Carmelite nun's spirit of prayer is a discernment based on an appreciation of characteristic stages of human and spiritual growth. Clearly the author has thought through the whole development of the spiritual life, and observed so many common traits in his spiritual direction, that he now sees Christian growth patterns in terms of an organic synthesis.

There are other signs that John sees a specific purpose for each step in the whole development process. He speaks of the benefits of the nights when he has already moved on to something better, and thus no longer feels the burden but the resulting joy. "One dark night, ...ah, the sheer grace!" "This glad night and purgation causes many benefits, even though to the soul it seemingly deprives it of them" (N, 1, 12, 1). This ability to see the overall picture also gives rise to the sometimes contrasting reactions of John and his directees, real or literary. Beginners rejoice in their initial consolations, but John is saddened by their lowly state. Those in the passive nights suffer, while John, knowing what is really happening, can rejoice.

A further sign of the presence of a system is John's continual use of parenthetical remarks to clarify what is happening. Some asides refer to what lies ahead (A, 2, 5, 1), others to stages already passed (F, 1, 18; C, Theme, 1)

Moreover, while focusing on the individual's return journey to God, John's system is not limited to this. He outlines for us the wonderful mystery of God's love in the Trinity, in history, through the Incarnation, brought to us in Jesus—all of this admirably presented in the "Romances," which need to be taken into account as the "downward" incarnational part of salvation history. "[The soul] knows, too, of the thousand other benefits by which she has been obligated to God from before the time of her birth" (C, 1, 1). The person journeying to union is aware of the love shown through the history of salvation. In fact, even in union, the Lord recalls and "communicates to her sweet mysteries of his Incarnation and of the ways of the redemption of humankind" (C, 23, 1).

John, then, is well aware of the system and stages of his own journey to union with the Lord. No doubt, many of his own directees were unaware of the systematic synthesis John had come to identify. To journey to God, it is not necessary to know the way ourselves, provided we have a guide. John laments the absence of suitable guides for so many persons that the Lord wants to advance (A, Prologue, 3).

Underlying John's vision is an appreciation of the inner life of love in the eternal Godhead, shared within the Trinity, and brought to birth in Jesus. This loving God now draws individuals to divine life through a series of identifiable stages. This process is not entirely predictable, nor identical for all, but if the guide knows the key moments in the journey, then those who seek God can be effectively guided to union.

Up to the time of John, Pseudo-Dionysius the Areopagite was the great authority in spiritual theology. His division of the spiritual journey into three stages was generally accepted: beginners, proficient, and perfect, corresponding to the purgative, illuminative, and unitive phases of spiritual growth. These three stages were considered important, but the transitions from one stage to another were not. John accepts this threefold division in his comments on the theme preceding stanza one of the *Canticle,* and refers to the purgative way in the *Ascent* (1, 1, 2–3). However, John introduces a new way of understanding the stages of spiritual growth.

Stages of Spiritual Growth in John's System

In his famous "Sketch of the Mount," John shows us the way to ascend Mount Carmel to find the Lord we seek. To the left and right of the sketch are two paths, designated "goods of heaven" and "goods of earth," *both* of which seem to be dead ends (though stylized versions by later artists often show one or both of these paths eventually meandering to the top). Only the narrow road in the middle—with its sevenfold *nada* ["nothing, nothing, nothing, nothing, nothing, nothing, and even on the Mount nothing"]—clearly reaches its goal, and is the quick way to divine union. John's diagram of the ascent is given here, with a translation.

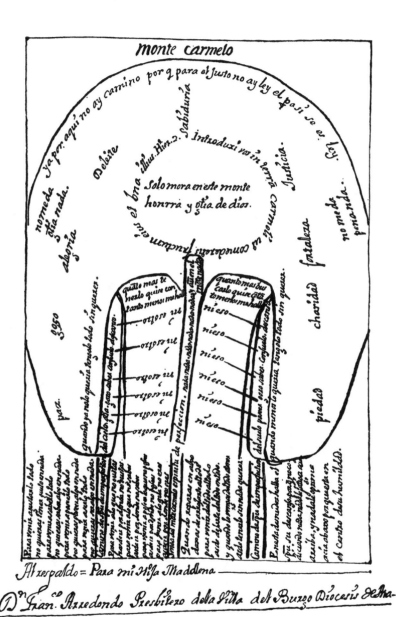

SKETCH OF MOUNT CARMEL BY ST. JOHN OF THE CROSS.

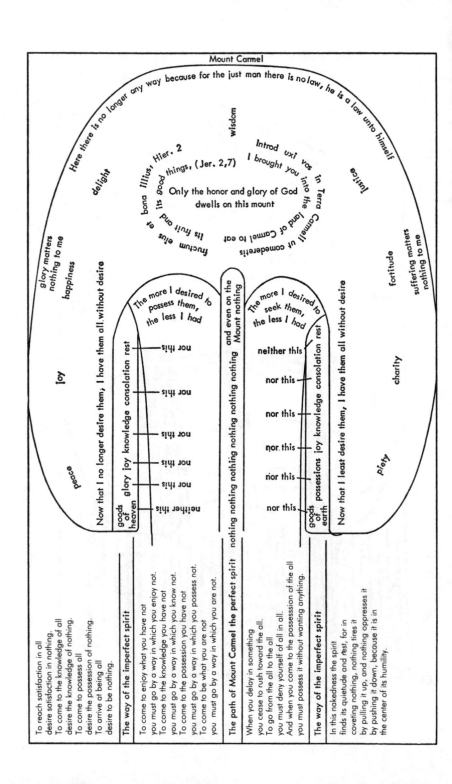

Mount Carmel

Here there is no longer any way because for the just man there is no law, he is a law unto himself

delight · happiness · glory matters nothing to me · joy · peace

wisdom · justice · fortitude · suffering matters nothing to me · charity · piety

et bona illius Hier. 2 — Introd uxi vos in Terra Carmeli ut comederetis — fructum eius et — its fruit and its good things, (Jer. 2,7)

Only the honor and glory of God dwells on this mount

The more I desired to possess them, the less I had

The more I desired to seek them, the less I had

and even on the Mount nothing

nothing nothing nothing nothing nothing

goods of heaven | glory joy knowledge consolation rest
nor this / nor this / nor this / nor this / nor this / neither this

goods of earth | possessions joy knowledge consolation rest
neither this / nor this / nor this / nor this / nor this / nor this

Now that I no longer desire them; I have them all without desire

Now that I least desire them, I have them all without desire

To reach satisfaction in all
desire satisfaction in nothing.
To come to the knowledge of all
desire the knowledge of nothing.
To come to possess all
desire the possession of nothing.
To arrive at being all
desire to be nothing.

The way of the imperfect spirit

To come to enjoy what you have not
you must go by a way in which you enjoy not.
To come to the knowledge you have not
you must go by a way in which you know not.
To come to the possession you have not
you must go by a way in which you possess not.
To come to be what you are not
you must go by a way in which you are not.

The path of Mount Carmel the perfect spirit

When you delay in something
you cease to rush toward the all.
To go from the all to the all
you must deny yourself of all in all.
And when you come to the possesssion of the all
you must possess it without wanting anything.

The way of the imperfect spirit

In this nakedness the spirit
finds its quietude and rest, for in
coveting nothing, nothing fires it
by pulling it up, and nothing oppresses it
by pushing it down, because it is in
the center of its humility.

Here is a simplified version:

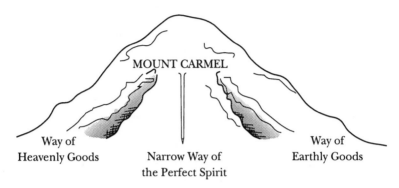

Way of
Heavenly Goods

Narrow Way of
the Perfect Spirit

Way of
Earthly Goods

The narrow *nada* path, in the middle of John's diagram, is the one that leads directly and speedily to the peak; that center path is not a smooth ascent, however, but has many ups and downs along the way. "The soul, if it desires to pay close attention, will clearly recognize how on this road it suffers many ups and downs, and how immediately after prosperity some tempest and trial follows, so much so that seemingly the calm was given to forewarn and strengthen it against the future penury" (N, 2, 18, 3). Classical spiritual writers prior to John had recognized the steps in the ascent and, as we have seen, portrayed the center path from base to peak as an arduous journey in three stages.

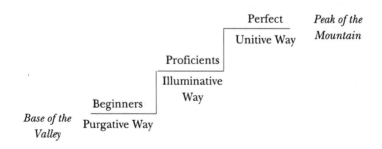

Writers before John generally considered these stages important, but seldom referred to the transitions from one to the other, considering them secondary and unimportant. Other authors referred to painful transitional experiences in which we seem to be separated from God by a "cloud of unknowing." Prior to John, both terminology and concepts were still fluid. His enormous experience in spiritual direction, together with his mature mystical experiences, enabled him to outline the stages better than anyone before him. Not only did John's Toledo experience bring personal growth by dying to himself, but he learned there that the painful experiences of life are often the moments of greatest grace and progress. John calls these painful transitional experiences "nights," and his terminology has remained. Thus, John modified the schema he inherited as follows:

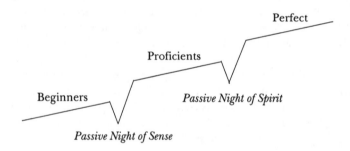

Thus, to the traditional schema of three "ways," John's system—seek God, through the nights, to union and renewal—adds a careful analysis of two crucial transitions. John says little about the "way" of beginners, and does not deal with them at length as an independent stage. Rather, since he believes that others have already said enough on the subject, his own discussions start with the night of sense. We only know what he thinks about the beginners' stage from parenthetical remarks in his writings, where he pauses to recall the way things used to be. By gathering together these comments, we realize that he considered beginners as a distinct stage, preceding the passive night of sense.

The stage of "proficiency" follows, the so-called "illuminative way," which for John it is a kind of plateau between the two passive nights. The passive night of spirit follows, and leads to the "unitive way" of the "perfect" (i.e., those who have been "perfected" by grace and union with God). This final stage is the goal of this life, and thus the most important phase in the process of growth, but the two passive nights or transitional phases are also major growth periods in John's system. The passive night of sense corresponds to the beginning of contemplation; the passive night of spirit is the decisive period of life, and leads to permanent transformation in God.

All of John's four major commentaries presuppose this schema, although it is most prominent in the *Ascent* and *Dark Night*. The *Canticle* presents the same journey in terms of the lover's search for her Beloved. The *Living Flame* deals primarily with the later phases of the journey, only retroactively mentioning earlier stages. The *Ascent of Mount Carmel* discusses the journey of faith and the individual's active role, first in the purification of sense, and later in the purification of the spirit. The *Dark Night* deals with the same journey, but highlights the passive components of the nights. We will consider the different stages in detail in the next chapter.

Before leaving the outline of John's system, we can mention that there are parallels between his stages and those of Teresa of Avila, although there are differences, too. In the *Interior Castle*, Teresa identifies seven stages in the spiritual life, which she describes in terms of seven inner "dwelling-places" or "mansions." (Earlier, in the *Book of Her Life*, Teresa had written of four stages, called the four waters; these four stages did not cover the whole journey, but only that part which Teresa had experienced by 1565, the date of the final version of her autobiography.)[45]

This simple overview of the stages and the accompanying sketches indicate the general outline of John's system. Of course, life is more complicated than an overview or a sketch, and richer too. However, a schema can be helpful when used with freedom and sensitivity.

The Seeker's Attitudes During the Journey

The journey to the mountaintop of union with God is full of darkness and trials (A, Prologue, 1), increased knowledge of one's own miseries, suffering, and distress (A, Prologue, 5). It is a journey in which seekers meet people "in the style of Job's comforters," proclaiming that their problems are due to "depression, or temperament, or to some hidden wickedness" (A, Prologue, 4). Other "friends" confidently announce that these seekers "are falling back since they finds no satisfaction or consolation as they previously did in the things of God" (A, Prologue, 5).

Some of those who could otherwise make the journey hamper God by their resistance; "they do not want to enter the dark night or allow themselves to be placed in it" (A, Prologue, 3). Others misunderstand what is happening to them and are harmed by unenlightened spiritual directors (A, Prologue, 4), or encumbered by attachment to consolations they receive (A, Prologue, 7).

Those who are ready for this journey have reached a new level of awareness about themselves and their relationship to God.[46] While feeling grateful and indebted to God, these individuals may feel "that God is angry and hidden" (C, 1, 1); yet they wish to search for God. It is no use beginning this journey unless the seeker really wants the union to which it leads. Such a one longs for union, and with "longings of love" "complains" of God's absence (C, 1, 2). The journey will require a deep longing for Christ, a strong determination, linked with enthusiasm, not stubbornness; this will lead to genuine happiness ((N, 1, Explanation, 2).

Human and religious growth requires a long time of slow maturing, and one of the key qualities needed in the journey up the mountain is patience.[47] Those who lack this virtue "grow angry with themselves in an unhumble impatience. So impatient are they about these imperfections that they want to become saints in a day" (N, 1, 5, 3). However, the required patience should not be separated from another essential virtue for this arduous journey, namely, a sense of urgency. In a passage that shows both his experience with many directees and his sense of humor, John says, "[Many beginners] do not have the patience to wait until God gives them what they need, when he so desires.... Some, however, are so patient about their desire for advancement that God would prefer to see them a little less so" (*ibid.*).

Thus, there are two indispensable attitudes that at first seem opposed; it is important to progress, and it is irresponsible to prolong unvirtuous patience. However, a searcher needs to patiently continue making an effort with steady enthusiasm even when apparently not getting anywhere. We can join together these two necessary and complementary qualities into one virtue for the journey, "patient-urgency." We need patience because the journey is long, but a mere patient acceptance of the passing of time is inadequate and will produce no magical effect. Rather, patience needs to be complemented by daily effort.

A key requirement for the journey is the use of means suitable for each stage. Once these means are identified by personal discernment or spiritual direction, we should persevere in their use. However, we can never become attached to the means themselves, a failing typical of those who journey along the wide paths of earthly or heavenly goods. Apparently spiritual practices can become the greatest self-deception of all, and even the best means can be absolutized and made into idols, thereby stunting further growth. Thus, the persevering use of suitable means must be complemented by flexibility in changing means when such a change becomes appropriate. Perseverance and flexibility are not mutually exclusive, but rather another bipolar attitude for the journey.

The difficult journey to the mountaintop of union involves purification from all that hinders union.[48] Those who journey must purify their selfish unwillingness to enter the night, and their fervent craving for success in the journey. Reading John helps us realize we can be attached to anything, including our own progress, experiences, consolations, motivations, holy desires, and even our spirit of sacrifice. All must be purified, for this journey requires "indifference," emptiness, openness to whatever God wants of us. Seekers thereby, "in peace and tranquility, continue to advance well" (A, Prologue, 7).

Once seekers have become aware of new relationships between themselves and God, and courageously and patiently commit themselves to journey to the mountaintop, they must learn to accept the human-divine reality that the narrow path of the *nadas* is the only road to the goal. So many Christians will try anything before what they know in their hearts is the one path guaranteed to lead to union. Many who seek alternatives carry in their hearts the nagging conviction that John is probably right.

The journey is frightening at times, and can be dreadful. However, searchers should know that they are not the main protagonist in this drama; God is. Strictly speaking, we do not journey by our own efforts to union with God. Rather, God in love and compassion draws us through the nights to a share in the divine life. Even in the dreadful moments that the journey may offer, we are not lost, or wandering aimlessly, but God is drawing us ever onward. This can be encouraging to individuals in their painful struggles.

Awareness of God's challenge, together with patience and urgency, perseverance and flexibility regarding means, constancy in accepting the sacrifices entailed in journeying along the narrow path, and unflinching desire for union, ready a person for this arduous climb. Faith will be challenged, but only persevering love will enable a person to endure the hardships of the journey. Laying aside superficial spiritualities with their shallow optimism and mediocre challenge, seekers who accept John's rigorous redirection of life to God will feel the exhilaration of arriving at the top and looking back over the extraordinary beauty of the climb they have made.

Guided by a Saint

I have always loved mountain climbing, and my experiences climbing in the Alps remind me of the ascetical demands of discipleship. My alpine mountain guide filled me with enthusiastic desire for the summit, taught me to rise early and to climb while fasting, not taking large strides when small steps would do. He insisted that I never stop but rather develop a rhythm in the climb, so that after a while climbing becomes automatic. I remember how often I wanted to pause, perhaps drink from a mountain stream, but my guide discouraged all digression, insisting that the peak alone merited our concentration. I found that you soon lose sight of the peak when climbing, as some shoulder of the mountain or an outcrop of rock intervenes, and you set your sights on each crest in the climb.

After but a little climbing, you lose sight of where you have come from and where you are going—the guide is particularly helpful at that time. I remember once taking four hours and twenty-five minutes to get part way up a glacier and, threatened by a storm, coming down in twenty minutes—how painfully slow to climb up, and how quick to lose the gains made! I have climbed alone, with a guide, or roped with six others. Sometimes the latter were helpful, as the members of the group aided each other, but I have also slipped hundreds of feet, dragged down by someone else I was tied to. Climbing is never easy, and no matter how much you think ahead about the climb, nothing substitutes for the real thing. But there are few experiences in life that compare with the thrill of reaching the summit, and people who have never endured the climb, and felt the exhilaration, have lost one of life's great gifts. When you have climbed to a significant peak you see the world below you in a way no one else can; but more significantly, the conquest of a climb helps you see life in a different way. I feel not only grateful but deeply indebted to my guide. As I think over those significant times, I am sitting in front of a blazing log fire in a campground. The day was tiring and exciting; the climb arduous and rewarding; the fire warm and transforming; the night is ahead. So many of John's images cascade before me.

John was an outstanding spiritual guide, who knew well the way to the top of Mount Carmel and the characteristics of both determined travelers and curious spiritual tourists. He was totally dedicated to the former, and all his works focus on their needs. Though aware of the latter, he does not ordinarily include them in his system. This should be constantly kept in mind when reading John, since readers frequently assume John is criticizing others, when in fact he is speaking of the faults of religiously dedicated people like themselves.

John warns all potential directees neither to presume that their experiences are equal to union with God, nor to conclude that God is absent from their lives if they are without special spiritual communications. "If a person experiences some elevated spiritual communication or feeling or knowledge, it should not be thought that the experiences are similar to the clear and essential vision or possession of God.... It should be known too that if all these sensible and spiritual communications are wanting and persons live in dryness, darkness, and dereliction, they must not think that God is any more absent than in the former case" (C, 1, 4). John had reason to dispute the high value placed on extraordinary experiences in his "Censure and Opinion on the Spirit and the Attitude in Prayer of a Discalced Carmelite Nun," and to encourage Doña Juana de Pedraza when she suffered from dryness (Letter 19).

John sees the dedicated individual as a special charge to the spiritual director. Such a "thirsting soul" is "the bride," and will find that "God...is hidden" within, where he must be sought with love (C, 1, 6). This soul, "most beautiful among all creatures," seeks God and his rewarding fullness but finds God to be ever elusive. John advises the anxious searcher, "your desired Beloved lives hidden within your heart" (C, 1, 9), and thus, he insists that one focus attention on the inner search. "And what else do you search for outside, when within yourself you possess your riches, delights, satisfactions, fullness, and kingdom—your Beloved whom you desire and seek?" (C, 1, 8). John fills people with the thrill of the quest and, knowing what lies ahead, encourages them to remember constantly that God is always present to them. "It brings special happiness to a person to understand that God is never absent, not even from a soul in mortal sin (and how much less from one in the state of grace)" (C, 1, 8).

Journeying to God within requires expert guides who are both enlightened and experienced (A, Prologue, 4). Those directors who lack the necessary skills harm their directees (A, Prologue, 3–5; 2, 18; F, 3, 27–62). Moreover, journeying without a guide, some individuals "work and tire themselves greatly, and yet go backwards" (A, Prologue, 7). John is an expert guide who brings to his direction years of spiritual guidance of others, together with a solid grasp of theology. He details the lot of beginners, proficients, and the perfect (A, 1, 1, 3), points out the weaknesses and strengths of each stage, and indicates signs to look for when someone is ready to move to a new stage (A, 2, 13–15; N, 1, 9). Moreover, we need only to read a few chapters of any of John's works to arrive at the firm conviction that this guide knows exactly what he is doing, and where and how he is leading his directees.

However, not only is John one of the most knowledgeable spiritual directors in the history of Christian spirituality, one who has influenced most succeeding syntheses, but his system claims our confidence for another reason: It produced a great saint. Excellent works of systematic theology can be produced by individuals who are themselves failures in their dedication to the Lord. Sanctity is not a requirement for an accurate understanding of academic theology. It is, however, for spiritual theology and mysticism. John guides searchers to God, and we need to be assured that his way is successful. John must not only be knowledgeable; he must be a saint. Great as he is, he never imposes his ideas on anyone. His humility toward his own insights reminds us not to be fundamentalists or literalists in our use of his vision and teaching.

Not only did John attain a high degree of personal holiness, as we have seen, but the church, on both the official and popular levels, has publicly recognized John as a model of Christian living. Canonizing saints is frequently a "politicized" process and can be used for purposes of control. Ideally, however, official recognition is complemented by widespread popular acclaim, and such is clearly the case with John. In fact, even those who are intimidated by John often have the nagging suspicion that he is right. Saints are God's gifts to the church, often channeling God's revelation in a vital way to complement magisterial teaching and theological reflection. Some saints simply embody perennial Christian values; others respond to specific situations or problems in the church. Sixteenth century Spain produced Ignatius of Loyola, Teresa of Avila, Peter of Alcántara, Francis Borgia and others. John differs from them all. His sanctity is molded by internal ecclesiastical persecution, as he strives for renewal and reform in the post-conciliar church after the Council of Trent (1545–1563).

Since his twenties John strove for a quality of life that religious institutions of his day rarely facilitated. He even considered withdrawing to a Carthusian monastery. But at Teresa's request, he dedicated himself to reform. His success, especially as a spiritual director at the Incarnation, led to others' jealousy, and spiteful superiors imprisoned him. Later in Toledo, he was humiliated, disgraced, and tormented by individuals convinced of their own rightness, who punished him with imprisonment and solitude, binding others to secrecy—an astounding story of religion's failure. Worse lay ahead, when his own disciples in the reform sought to limit his influence, push him out of leadership, and degrade him in the way ostensibly religious people have of attacking their own, even those who are carefully obedient and orthodox.

Through all his hardships, John maintained his values, strove after his unchanging goals, and never became like his persecutors nor succumbed to bitterness. He came through it all an extraordinary human being, who achieved his goals without trampling on anyone, without abusing the power religion gives, and without reducing the ideals he had maintained from his youth.

Today religion is too often linked with power, control, and money. Essential values are sacrificed for the maintenance of institutional power, and pseudo-leaders trample over the dedicated in the name of religious authority. Individuals who take a different path are often persecuted, especially when they have a large following. Ecclesiastical totalitarianism raises its head again, and mysticism is left to a courageous few.

A saint for our times, an exceptional guide, the era of the greatest influence of the Mystical Doctor is ahead of us.

CHAPTER FOUR

Stages in the Journey

Beginners

John of the Cross focuses his skills as a spiritual director on those Christians who have made a determined commitment to give their lives to the Lord. His own life situation and most of his work was with religious. John gives no attention to "pre-evangelization" or to the early stages of catechetical and spiritual training.

Moreover, for John as for most spiritual writers, the term "beginners" means those dedicated individuals who have already resolutely decided to direct their lives to God; they have already begun the journey, even though their good will needs the guiding help of a spiritual director. Therefore, "beginners" for John refers to those who already have a certain degree of dedication (at least compared with their former state of alienation from God)—they have started the journey to perfection and Christian maturity. However, John shows little concern for this group in his writing, and does not discuss it at any length as a separate stage in the spiritual journey (except briefly in Book One of the *Ascent* and the early chapters of the *Night*).[49] As some physicians are surgeons and some general practitioners—both accomplishing noble tasks —John is not a general practitioner but a specialist in the later stages of the spiritual life.

Yet although John begins his writings at the point where individuals enter the passive night of sense and initial contemplation, he sometimes refers in passing to the earlier stage that his directees have fortunately left behind. Gathering together John's scattered asides, we can determine reasonably accurately what he thought of this earliest stage.

John often speaks critically of this stage of the spiritual life, generally referring to it as the life of sense. Beginners "resemble children who kick and cry, and struggle to walk by themselves when their mothers want to carry them; in walking by themselves they make no headway, or if they do, it is at a child's pace" (A, Prologue, 3). For pedagogical reasons, John writes negatively of this period of remote preparation, hoping that his criticisms will encourage people to move beyond and enter willingly into the purifying night of sense. He hopes to "help beginners understand the feebleness of their state" (N, 1, 1, 1), and "how very similar their deeds are to those of children" (N, 1, 1, 3).

Using as his basis the seven capital sins, understood in a spiritual sense, John first notes that beginners are proud of their own progress and achievements. "A certain kind of secret pride is generated in them that begets a complacency with themselves and their accomplishments" (N, 1, 2, 1). They publicize their own growth, are intolerant of others' lack of devotion, and when criticized "quickly search for some other spiritual advisor more to their liking, someone who will congratulate them and be impressed by their deeds" (N, 1, 2, 3). They become attached to their devotion, thereby turning it into a vice. Embarrassed by, or oblivious to, their own failures, they become insincere in dealing with others, overanxious about what others think of them, and reluctant to see good in others.

The pride of beginners leads to spiritual avarice. Their attachment and possessiveness of heart centers on "hearing counsels," "learning spiritual maxims," and accumulating religious objects. Nowadays, for example, this spiritual avarice can lead beginners to an attendance at innumerable prayer workshops, the needless accumulation of books on prayer, and the constant comfort and consolation of ever longer retreats and workshops.

Beginners have numerous imperfections, "many of which can be called spiritual lust" (N, 1, 4, 1). Sometimes "the origin of these rebellions is the devil" (N, 1, 4, 3), but at other times they may simply "proceed from the pleasure human nature finds in spiritual exercises" (N, 1, 4, 1), since our physical body naturally participates in our soul's delights. However, beginners can easily become attached to the accompanying physical pleasure. "Some people are so delicate that when gratification is received spiritually, or from prayer, they immediately experience a lust that so inebriates them and caresses their senses that they become as it were engulfed in the delight and satisfaction of that vice" (N, 1, 4, 5). As attachment to these feelings increases, "the soul will grow cold in the love of God" (N, 1, 4, 7).

Beginners easily become angry, either at the loss of their own consolations, or at other people's imperfections, or at their own lack of growth. "Many of these beginners make numerous plans and great resolutions, but...the more resolves they make the more they break, and the greater becomes their anger" (N, 1, 5, 3).

Spiritual gluttony is also a common failing of beginners. Some manifest spiritual gluttony in seeking only the comfort, consolation, and satisfaction that involvement in the spiritual life can bring. "All their time is spent looking for satisfaction and spiritual consolation" (N, 1, 6, 6).

Two other weaknesses follow from those already mentioned, namely spiritual envy and sloth. Beginners often become dissatisfied with the comfort they experience and are envious at anyone else's spiritual growth. Moreover, emphasis on the consolations that sometimes accompany the early stages of spiritual growth leads beginners to a distaste for the unpleasant sacrifices needed to advance. "Because of their sloth, they subordinate the way of perfection...to the pleasure and delight of their own will" (N, 1, 7, 3).

Three positive features of this stage of preparation are religious fervor, prayer, and mortification. Beginners are enthusiastic about their dedication to the Lord, and find great satisfaction in it. They enjoy long periods of prayer, are pleased with themselves when they practice penance, and love the consolations and comforts of religion. "The soul finds its joy, therefore, in spending lengthy periods at prayer, perhaps even entire nights; its penances are pleasures; its fasts, happiness; and the sacraments and spiritual conversations are its consolations" (N, 1, 1, 3). Elsewhere, John says beginners are like new wine, heady and bubbly. "These beginners feel so fervent and diligent in their spiritual exercises and undertakings" (N, 1, 2, 1), that their spiritual life seems to them like a thrilling adventure.

Part of the religious fervor of beginners is their dedication to prayer. "The practice of beginners is to meditate and make acts and discursive reflection with the imagination" (F, 3, 32). They spend much time in prayer, often basing it on scenes from Scripture. Their prayer is discursive, a "work through images, forms, and figures" (A, 2, 13, 1). Although this is not the quality of prayer John seeks to engender in his directees, it is good for beginners, and therefore it is important not to abandon it too soon, "so that there is no regression" (*ibid.*). Discursive meditations are remote means for beginners, and help them to dispose themselves for more spiritual interests. "By these sensitive means beginners dispose their spirit and habituate it to spiritual things, and at the same time they void their senses of all other base, temporal, secular, and natural forms and images" (*ibid.*).

This prayer of beginners today often takes forms different from those in John's time. Traditional Western methods of formal meditation, with their various steps and their recommended use of the imagination and discursive reflection, are now supplanted by books, radio, and television. Though formal meditation on biblical scenes was once the universal preparation for prayer, today reflective and dedicated persons may undergo similar preparation through reading, listening, and viewing the pains of humanity and the tragedies of a sinful world. The prayer of many beginners today consists in "just being quiet in the presence of God." This quiet, affective, centered prayer is often confused with contemplation, but it is the beginning, not the end, of the journey.

In addition to religious fervor and meditation, the third positive characteristic of beginners is the practice of external mortification. John sees the basis of this in an imitation of Christ. He suggests moderation in the exercise of our external senses, recommends that his directees temper their love of ease by seeking that which is difficult, and urges them to mortify pride by acting, thinking, and speaking poorly of themselves (A, 1, 13, 9). These recommendations of John have often given him a bad reputation among modern men and women, who find such suggestions repugnant. However, two points should be kept in mind: first, this apparent negativity needs to be seen in light of the renewal and growth that John seeks; and second, John spoke this way at a time when religion often viewed earthly realities as not directly connected with religious growth. This latter view, radically modified by Vatican II's theology of earthly realities, could today be reinterpreted as an attitude of self-education in integrating all values into one unified self-gift to God.

Fervor, meditation, and mortification are the points John identifies as the beginning of a great future. In our time we should look for approaches to life that embody similar attitudes. What would be the corresponding characteristics today? What are today's signs that the necessary attitudes are present? We are not concerned here with "pre-beginners" who are frequently slaves to duty or authority, and attached to externals of correct performance. Some writers suggest, for example, that those well-intentioned Christians who constantly desire to adapt liturgical and ecclesiastical externals to their own temperaments are like John's "spiritual beginners." They seem unable to deny themselves anything for the sake of love alone; they lack an ability to really choose; they show inconstancy in their own duties; and their attitude toward the externals of faith is often childish. Some of these signs are negative, but the increased attention to religious matters is a step forward. It shows that the individual is thinking in a new way, but also needs guidance to enter the night ahead.

Night of Sense

There are two great "nights" in the spiritual journey, each of which has both an active and a passive dimension. "One night of purgation is sensory, by which the senses are purged and accommodated to the spirit.... The sensory night is common and happens to many" (N, 1, 8, 1).[50] The first night leads into the state of contemplation (A, 1, 1, 3); moreover, "not much time ordinarily passes after the initial stages of their spiritual life before beginners start to enter this night of sense" (N, 1, 8, 4). John begins his major writings with this night, which consists of an active reeducation of senses and a passive purification that comes in contemplation.

John neither despises the suitable objects of sensory experience nor the appropriate exercise of senses. In fact, he is one of the few mystics who insists that for those who reach the state of union even the senses are renewed in the enjoyment of their natural objects (A, 3, 20, 2). Thus, senses are not destroyed or put to death (as the etymology of the word "mortification" might seem to imply), but reeducated and redirected to God. This night of sense consists in the purification of disordered voluntary appetites (or desires) that crave inappropriate sensory satisfaction, for not every desire is an obstacle to growth. "The appetites are not all equally detrimental, nor are all equally a hindrance to the soul" (A, 1, 11, 2). In many cases, "a soul can easily experience them in its sensitive nature and yet be free of them in the rational part of its being" (*ibid.*). So John is urging self-control of those habitual voluntary appetites that impede union with God. He does not include occasional involuntary desires to which the individual does not consent. "Now it is true that the sensory peceptions of hearing, sight, smell, taste, and touch are unavoidable; yet they will no more hinder a soul—if it denies them—than if they were not experienced" (A, 1, 3, 4). The active night of sense, the purification of attachments to the objects of sense, begins with an habitual desire to imitate Christ. While traditional Christian asceticism has sometimes distorted the biblical image of Jesus, nevertheless renunciation of all sensory satisfaction that is not for the honor and glory of God remains part of Jesus' message. John gives a series of maxims that bring harmony and tranquillity to the "four natural passions" of joy, hope, fear, and sorrow (A, 1, 13, 6; see also A, 1, 13, 9). These maxims complement the recommendations written on the bottom of his sketch of Mount Carmel (A, 1, 13, 11).

This active purification of the appetites "is the requirement for entering the happy night of the senses" (N, 1, 8, 4). John offers three signs that, when simultaneously present, indicate that seekers are entering the passive night of sense, which is contemplation.[51] First, they cease to find any consolation, either from creatures or from the things of God. Second, they are pained by their own lack of service to God (N, 1, 9). Third, these persons can no longer meditate as before, and have no desire to apply the imagination to formal discursive meditation, but rather find satisfaction in a quiet, loving attention toward God (A, 2, 13, 2–4).[52] When these signs are present together, these individuals should leave meditation without fear and follow the Spirit, for God is leading them from meditation to contemplation (N, 1, 10, 1).

Many suffer at this time from the loss of the security and satisfaction of their previously successful meditations. Sometimes they strive unsuccessfully to return to their discursive prayer and "consequently impair God's work and do not profit by their own" (N, 1, 10, 1). Rather, purifying their attachment to meditation, these individuals need willingly to remain empty in times of prayer, "content simply with a loving and peaceful attentiveness to God" (N, 1, 10, 4), letting God fill their emptiness if God so wishes. In the meantime, cultivating detachment, humility, and charity, they should leave all else to God, who "introduces people into this night to purge their senses and accommodate, subject, and unite the lower part of the soul to the spiritual part by darkening it and causing a cessation of discursive meditation" (N, 1, 11, 3). This redirection of the desires is part of a process of integration, whereby our inner fragmentation is overcome and all aspects of our human existence are brought together in a self-gift to God. This centered life (or purity of heart, as Scripture calls it) is the singlemindedness and singleheartedness necessary to make this journey courageously to the summit of Mount Carmel.

In addition to the effort-filled dedication to conquer our self-centeredness and focus our desires on God alone, individuals must willingly surrender to God's purifying activity in prayer.[53] "When the appetite has been fed somewhat and has become in a certain fashion accustomed to spiritual things and has acquired some fortitude and constancy, God begins to wean the soul, as they say, and place it in the state of contemplation" (F, 3, 32). Having controlled our own prayer for so long, we must now let God take control. Initial contemplation shows the typical characteristics of contemplative prayer. It is not merely an exercise in faith, but an experience of God, in which the individual communes with God through a loving knowledge. "Since God, then, as the giver communes with individuals through a simple, loving knowledge, they also, as the receivers, commune with God through a simple and loving knowledge or attention" (F, 3, 34). The purifying illumination that comes in contemplation "is received passively in the soul according to the supernatural mode of God, and not according to the natural mode of the soul"

(F, 3, 34). An experience of God's presence, contemplation includes an intuition that is intense, profound, and very simple. "God...secretly and quietly inserts in the soul loving wisdom and knowledge" (F, 3, 33). This immediate and direct contact with God is an ineffable, indescribable experience, not through images and words, but in love.

This "passive" purification through contemplative prayer is given in different ways and degrees particularly to those who are already being purified through the active night of sense.

> Not everyone undergoes this in the same way, neither are the temptations identical....
>
> Those who have more considerable capacity and strength for suffering, God purges more intensely and quickly. But those who are very weak he keeps in this night for a long time. Their purgation is less intense and their temptations abated, and he frequently refreshes their senses to keep them from backsliding. (N, 1, 14, 5)

Some individuals never reach union because "they are never wholly in the night or wholly out of it" (*ibid.*). Those who are willing to accept the purifying trials of the night receive many blessings and discover that the night has many sanctifying qualities (N, 1, 12–14): knowledge of self and an ability to recognize the truth about one's weaknesses; knowledge of God and divine grandeur with an ability to commune more respectfully with God; conquest of spiritual pride that leads to spiritual humility; love of neighbor, and greater submissiveness and obedience in one's journeying to God. The individual overcomes the prior weaknesses of spiritual avarice, lust, and gluttony. Dwelling in spiritual peace and tranquillity, the individual increasingly exercises virtue, becomes gentle and charitable toward others, and acquires liberty of spirit and singleminded dedication to God.

A Plateau Period of Consolidation

Spiritual writers prior to John considered the stage of proficients an important period in Christian growth, but John views it as a plateau between the two chasms of the passive nights of sense and spirit. It is an opportunity to regather one's energies after the hardships of the night of sense, and to grow in a different way. "If His Majesty intends to lead the soul on, he does not put it in this dark night of spirit immediately after its going out from the aridities and trials of the first purgation and night of sense" (N, 2, 1, 1).

The stage between the nights is a very positive phase, peaceful and satisfying. "In this new state, as one liberated from a cramped prison cell, [the soul] goes about the things of God with much more freedom and satisfaction of spirit and with more abundant interior delight than it did in the beginning before entering the night of sense" (*ibid.*). The individual in this stage of "proficients" is beyond the distractions of the faculties previously experienced in discursive prayer, readily finds God in profound recollection and initial contemplation, and sometimes is called to the prayer of quiet. Such persons know their lives have changed; filled with confident love of God and love of sacrifice, they also show an increased service of others, detachment from what is not conducive to a life with God, and personal renewal. Moreover, "the delight and interior gratification that these proficients enjoy abundantly and readily is communicated more copiously to them than previously and consequently overflows into the senses more than was usual before the sensory purgation" (N, 2, 1, 2). An individual can spend many years in this pleasing stage punctuated only infrequently by previews of the remaining purification needed, "like omens or messengers of the coming night of spirit" (*ibid.*), reminders that the first night only began the process.

Although the night of sense is painful, it is only a temporary and partial remedy to one's rooted attachment to false values, like "cutting off a branch" rather than "pulling up roots" (N, 2, 2, 1). The night of sense accommodates the senses to the spirit, rather than completing the person's union with God. What still lies ahead is the entire remaking and transformation of the person through the three theological virtues, the means of spiritual purification. But before this dreadful night of spirit, the individual benefits from the commitment shown in facing the trial of the night of sense. The virtuous life, serene contemplation, and interior satisfaction that the

proficient experiences are not simply the product of the restful plateau experience, but are the fruit of the achievements in the night
of sense. Rather than originating in the former, they result from the
latter.

The partial healing of the senses in the first night is inadequate, and although proficients experience God in a new way,
many imperfections still remain. These roots of sinful appetites burden these seekers with "a distracted and inattentive spirit" that
causes a "natural dullness" towards the life of the spirit (N, 2, 2, 2).

Proficients can also become attached to the blessings of this
period. Having lived in dryness for so long, the refreshing renewal
and partial contemplative experience of God seem like the end of
the road, and individuals are easily tempted to cling to what they
begin to think they have earned.

This is the period, John says, when seekers may experience vi-
sions, raptures, and other delightful spiritual feelings (N, 2, 2, 3).
Since these gifts often cause pleasant reactions in the senses, or may
bring one a reputation for holiness, some become allured by the
gratifying reaction. Sometimes the same blessings provoke self-de-
lusions regarding one's progress, and even vanity and arrogance.
John also suggests that a further danger is a too familiar attitude to
God. "They become audacious with God and lose holy fear, which is
the key to and guardian of all the virtues" (N, 2, 2, 3). Even genu-
inely spiritual people, with extraordinary spiritual gifts, can be led
astray.

Although this period is the most spiritually rewarding an individual has so far experienced on the journey to union, John affirms
that "these proficients are still very lowly and natural in their communion with God" (N, 2, 3, 3). And speaking further of their fail-
ings, he adds "that no proficients, however strenuous their efforts,
will avoid many of these natural affections and imperfect habits" (N,
2, 2, 4).

The greatest danger for proficients is attachment to the new
and deeper spiritual experiences they are now enjoying after the
trials of the first night; they should prepare instead for the night
ahead. Seekers must now be willing to let go of even these seemingly
more spiritual pleasures, and risk the emptiness through which they
will be wholly drawn to God.

The Night of the Spirit

The purifying night of the senses is a partial redirection of their energies. However, "evil habits reside in the spirit and until these habits are purged, the senses cannot be completely purified of their rebellions and vices" (N, 2, 3, 1). The second night, essentially focused on the spiritual faculties, also uproots the remaining imperfections of the sensory appetites and desires. The night of spirit is both active and passive. The active night consists in an individual's efforts to purify the spiritual faculties—intellect, memory, and will—of their false or limited contents and methods of knowing God. "The theological virtues...cause the same emptiness and darkness in their respective faculties: faith in the intellect, hope in the memory, and charity in the will" (A, 2, 6, 1). Though created things may give us some remote knowledge of their creator, we do not come to learn more about God by increased use of the intellect, accumulating as many facts as possible on an individual and community level. Rather, we come to a deeper personal knowledge of God by denying the intellect its natural object and opening ourselves to the revealing vision of faith. "The light of faith in its abundance suppresses and overwhelms that of the intellect. For the intellect, by its own power, extends only to natural knowledge" (A, 2, 3, 1). Thus, more is known of God by letting go of our preconceptions to receive the light of faith, even though this illumination causes darkness to the intellect. Not only do sensory images mislead us regarding God, insofar as we imagine that God is somehow like them, but so too can the accumulated natural knowledge of the intellect. Primitives may have carved their god from wood or stone, but moderns carve their god from ideas, theories, information. Both are idols, and the dark night of faith purifies the intellect of attachment to its natural objects and urges the disciple to be open to the knowledge that faith gives. "However impressive may be one's knowledge or experience of God, that knowledge or experience will have no resemblance to God and amount to very little" (A, 2, 4, 3).[54]

Similarly, we do not come closer to the true vision of the compassionate God simply by accumulating memories of certain past instances of divine love for us, individually or collectively, and assuming that God's mercy can go no further. Memory comes to possess

God by denying itself its own natural function and by turning in hope to the divinely promised future. "Thus, if it is true—as indeed it is— that the soul must journey by knowing God through what he is not rather than through what he is, it must journey, insofar as possible, by way of the denial and rejection of natural and supernatural apprehensions. This is our task now with the memory" (A, 3, 2, 3). So the memory refuses to rest not only in recollection of all sensory objects, but also in previous images and experiences of God. Those who do not purify their memories end by worshipping a god created from their own past experiences, which are always limited and in need of healing. While this purification may mean letting go of some fine memories of God's past favors, John considers the purity of mind and heart more helpful to union than clinging to the past, since God is always ready to give us more (A, 3, 3, 4).

Those who resist hope's purification of the memory suffer the consequences of being constantly tied to the past, resubjected to previous imperfections, tempted by diabolical deceit, and deprived of the peace that detachment from our memories can bring (A, 3, 3–5). This purification of the memory is rewarding, for it causes inner tranquillity, disposes individuals for divine wisdom and virtues, frees them from temptations, and readies them for the influence of the Holy Spirit (A, 3, 6).

The third spiritual faculty that must be purified is the will. "We would have achieved nothing by purging the intellect and memory in order to ground them in the virtues of faith and hope had we neglected the purification of the will through charity" (A, 3, 16, 1). Since the will directs all the person's faculties, appetites, and passions, it is the spiritual faculty most responsible for disintegration or integration. By controlling the objects of the four passions—joy, hope, sorrow, and fear—the will can "keep the strength and ability of the soul for God, and direct it toward him" (A, 3, 16, 2). Relating all joy, hope, sorrow, and fear to the things of God, and by uniting these passions in a singleminded commitment to God, the multiple desires of life become one unique longing for God. Since any one of these passions, left uncontrolled, will always affect the other three, it is crucial that the individual deliberately make an effort in this active night of spirit to purify the disintegration caused by satisfying the will in many different and divergent objects. "When the will directs these faculties, passions, and appetites toward God, turning them away from all that is not God, the soul preserves its strength for God, and comes to love him with all its might" (*ibid.*). Desiring only what God desires, or desiring and loving everything in God, the individual comes to fulfill the challenge of Scripture: "You shall love the Lord, your God, with all your heart, and with all your soul, and with all your strength" (Dt 6:5).

Thus, "in order to journey to God the intellect must be perfected in the darkness of faith, the memory in the emptiness of hope, and the will in the nakedness and absence of every affection" (A, 2, 6, 1). In this active night of spirit, seekers do whatever they can to purify all their knowledge, memories, and desires, and direct their lives exclusively to God in faith, hope, and love.

Before the final stage of transforming union, the person must be cleansed of everything that is not of God, and the most rigorous part of this divine purification is the passive night of spirit, a special contemplative phase that both purifies and illumines. "This contemplation annihilates, empties, and consumes all the affections and imperfect habits the soul contracted throughout its life" (N, 2, 6, 5). The dark contemplation of the passive night of spirit brings a knowledge of God completely permeated with love. Individuals in this state lose the tranquil, partial communion experienced in the stage of proficients. They may feel that God has rejected them, and this feeling produces extreme pain, like that experienced by Job (N, 2, 5, 5). Not only do they feel empty, but they see more clearly their own misery and sin and feel unworthy of God and of all creatures (*ibid.*). Convinced that they will never be worthy, they begin to feel that they will never again possess the former blessings. "Under the stress of this oppression and weight, individuals feel so far from all favor that they think...there is no one who will take pity on them" (N, 2, 5, 7). Constantly faced with their own failures these individuals feel immersed in their own spiritual death.[55] Convinced of being rejected by God and by all friends, they are oppressed by their poverty, misery, helplessness, and abandonment. To the present overwhelming pain, and the uncertainty that any remedy will arise, is added the remembrance of past prosperity in the spiritual life, lost through no fault of their own. "They suspect that they are lost and that their blessings are gone forever" (N, 2, 9, 7). Immersed in the pain of the night, they experience profound helplessness, because there is so little they can do. Moreover, "individuals in this state find neither consolation nor support in any doctine or spiritual master" (N, 2, 7, 3).

During this dark trial, which "will last for some years, no matter how intense it may be" (N, 2, 7, 4), the seekers experience an inability to think of God, and "can neither pray vocally nor be attentive to spiritual matters, nor still less attend to temporal affairs and business" (N, 2, 8, 1). The contemplative illumination causing this "darkness" is permeated with love, but this increased love for God further intensifies the pain, since they feel completely powerless to pursue and encounter God. Although God becomes so important that all else seems a waste of time, the frustration at their inability to think of God or receive the peace they formerly enjoyed only augments the pain this night brings.

This night is the beginning of an extraordinary knowledge of God, a divine self-communication permeated with love. But while experiencing it, a person "feels very vividly indeed the shadow of death, the sighs of death, and the sorrows of hell, all of which reflect the feeling of God's absence, of being chastised and rejected by him, and of being unworthy of him, as well as the object of his anger" (N, 2, 6, 2).

The beneficial effects of the passive night include a new knowledge of God, unlike the limited images and concepts of the senses and spiritual faculties. This knowledge is linked to love, not yet the love of transforming union, but the love of urgent longing for life with God. This love makes us "bold enough to go out to be joined with God" (N, 2, 13, 9). Furthermore, the experience cleanses us, cures the roots of our evil, gives us accurate self-knowledge and perspective on our relationship to God.

Through the pain and darkness of this night individuals who seek union with God receive the purification and illumination that prepares them for the union with the Lord they seek.[56]

Union and Renewal

The goal of the spiritual journey is union with God, a union that also causes the transformation of one's entire personality.[57] The union that crowns the spiritual journey is not the "substantial union" whereby God sustains all created things in existence. Rather, the union experienced at the end of the journey is a supernatural transforming union that "exists when God's will and the soul's are in conformity, so that nothing in the one is repugnant to the other" (A, 2, 5, 3). Since this union is found only when there is a likeness of love, John calls it "the union of likeness" (*ibid.*). This likeness or conformity of will is attained through the purifications of the nights, after which the intellect, memory, will, appetites, and all movements of the person are united with God. "Accordingly, the intellect of this soul is God's intellect; its will is God's will; its memory is the eternal memory of God; and its delight is God's delight.... [It] has become God through participation in God" (F, 2, 34). So, a soul in this state of union is not moved by its own former passions, appetites, and natural inclinations, but "inclines and moves toward God in the first movements of its intellect, memory, will, and appetites, because of the great help and stability it has in God and its perfect conversion toward him" (C, 27, 7).

The love that leads us to center our entire life on God and in conformity with all God wills, culminates in a union so profound, John calls it "spiritual marriage," "a total transformation in the Beloved" (C, 22, 3).[58] The seeker can now recite the words of the "Spiritual Canticle":

> Now I occupy my soul
> and all my energy in his service;
> I no longer tend the herd,
> nor have I any other work
> now that my every act is love. (C, 28)

In this loving union, the individual is integrally dedicated to God who now understands, hopes, and loves *in* the seeker. Although longing for total union, which is not possible in this life, the individual is not frustrated but, in this too, lovingly conforms to God's will. John suggests that this habitual union becomes so intense on occasion that those in this state momentarily experience "actual union," caused by the powerful overflow into actual awareness of the same Holy Trinity who "inhabits the soul by divinely illuminating its intellect with the wisdom of the Son, delighting its will in the Holy Spirit, and by absorbing it powerfully and mightily in the delightful embrace of the Father's sweetness" (F, 1, 15).

Once this union of likeness is attained in spiritual marriage, the Lord himself rejoices together with those who have attained this stage (C, 22).[59] Their mutual love is so intense that the Lord reveals his plans of salvation to the espoused soul (C, 23). This loving union produces virtues in the spouse, and the gift of living them with constancy. Their mutual love, furthermore, produces peace (C, 24). In this experience of union the spouse rejoices in favors personally received, and also given so generously to others (C, 25). The transforming love of this union produces disinterest in whatever is not of God, and keeps all the desires in order. John alludes to seven degrees of this union, according to the seven gifts of the Holy Spirit (C, 26). Spiritual marriage implies a mutual surrender between God and the spouse (C, 27), attained by occupying one's entire being exclusively in the service of the Lord; "everything I do, I do with love, and everything I suffer, I suffer with the delight of love" (C, 28, 8). John affirms that the quality of this loving union is more sanctifying, and of greater value to the church, than many works of service and ministry done without such love (C, 29). This union brings intense peace, growth in virtue, and fruitfulness (C, 30); it is a mutual commitment, binding God and the human person to each other in a transformational experience that still preserves the individuality of each one (C, 31).[60] This state is entirely a gift from the Lord (C, 32), whose presence cleanses, graces, enriches, and illumines (C, 33); it involves an inestimable experience of indescribable love for the spouse (C, 34), that even brings delight to the Lord (C, 35). The mutual love of this union longs to reach fulfillment (C, 36) in the union of eternity (C, 37), which will further enrich the spouse and bring glory to the Lord whose grace has wrought this transformation (C, 38). Describing this eternal enrichment (C, 39), the spouse, transformed and at peace, longs for the final union in the loving transformation of eternal life (C, 40).

This final stage of spiritual marriage is "the highest degree of perfection one can reach in this life" (F, Prologue, 3), but the love of this final stage "can grow deeper in quality" and "become more ardent" (*ibid.*). Thus, while referring to the same stage as the later stanzas of the *Canticle,* the *Living Flame* comments on the increased intensity of love possible in this final transformation.

One quality of this loving union is that the spouse experiences being "forcefully transformed in God" (F, 1, 1). As our activity is taken over by the Holy Spirit, we yearn for fullness of eternal love, and so we pray, "Tear the veil of mortal life now" (*ibid.*). The longing for eternal union is one aspect of this experience of mutual love.

Another dimension, or intensification, of this unitive love is that individuals become aware of "how the three Persons of the Most Blessed Trinity, the Father, the Son, and the Holy Spirit, are the ones who effect this divine work of union" (F, 2, 1). They transform the spouse, changing death to life. Thus, a profound experience of the transforming love of the Trinity is a second aspect of this life of mutual love.

This love of union is illuminating, as God loves the seeker with the full force of each divine attribute. In this intense mutual loving and self-communication, God reveals the divine nature vitally through the attributes, as the spouse personally experiences the love, wisdom, goodness, mercy, and power of God.

Finally, the spouse experiences all creatures in God, through the overflowing love of this union, that produces "an awakening of God in the soul, effected in gentleness and love" (F, 4, 2). This knowledge of the essence of God, and of creation through its creator, is further enriched when God breathes into his loved one the excellent and delicate love and life of the Holy Spirit.

Growth Through Crisis

We have dealt with John's understanding of the stages in spiritual growth. He starts with the traditional outline of spiritual development in three stages, or "ways": purgative, illuminative, and unitive, corresponding to beginners, proficients, and the perfect, respectively. However, while the two transitional phases between these stages were of little importance to former spiritual theologians, they become essential to John's teaching. In fact, by commenting on John's fivefold development, we could miss his synthesis. John's many asides give us an idea of what he thought of the beginners' stage, but this is not an important stage for him, and it is mentioned simply because it is the point of departure. The stage of proficients is also comparatively unimportant, since the most significant growth does not take place there. The enrichment experienced during this plateau period is the result of a dedicated handling of the night of sense, and the growth caused by a deeper contemplative encounter with God. This parenthesis of the illuminative way, though sometimes marked by extraordinary experiences, may be called a time of consolidation and relative ease. Any growth that takes place here is not caused by this stage as such, but by continuing to apply the lessons learned in the previous stage. For John, it might be said that the deepest purgation and most powerful illumination both occur in the passive nights.

As he himself suggests in the second chapter of Book One of the *Ascent,* John's system can be summarized under three headings: the point of departure, the means to attain the end, and the goal of union (whence, how, and whither). His originality is in his understanding of the means. In fact, the two nights of sense and spirit are really conjoined in one great night of total development—the journey of love-permeated faith.

While accepting that time and patience are needed for mature growth, John also conveys a sense of urgency. We must grow! This growth takes place principally if not exclusively in the nights, the transitions or crisis periods of life. This growth is grounded in our knowledge of God, not attained positively by the accumulation of more facts *about* God, but rather negatively by emptying ourselves so that we never confine God to our own narrow views, but let God be who God wishes to be for us.

In choosing the narrow path of darkness and self-emptying, we make a love-directed choice of the unknown God. This choice involves letting go of our memories, past understandings, and experiences. However, in John, renunciation is never negative, but a choice in love for a better encounter. John's simple system is an exodus; a reaffirmation of the essentially paschal aspect of Christian growth.

Most people will not live these stages in precisely the way John presents them, nor does he think they will. God is the principal agent, drawing each individual toward union in divine life, with a loving respect for the individuality of each. Therefore modern spiritual directors should appreciate the great flexibility of John's system.

Growth takes place most of all in the crisis moments of life. Individuals who seek God need not know in which stage they are living, although their directors ought to have some inkling. Rather, individuals, appreciating John's basic insight, can face every minor crisis of each day with an awareness of its potential to produce growth. Each one's individual exodus to the promised land of union must pass through the trials of the desert. John's journey of negation and detachment is the contemporary journey of positive integration that brings the whole of life together in one great forward movement of loving dedication to God.

CHAPTER FIVE

The Person in the System of
John of the Cross

Human Fulfillment in John's Life and System

One of the major characteristics of the last quarter century is undoubtedly the ceaseless search for personal, corporate, and institutional development, fulfillment, and ongoing progress. This is as much a characteristic of selfish and exploitative individuals and corporations as it is of religiously dedicated individuals and ecclesial groups. The aspiration for fulfillment is an essential component of human life, and since Paul VI's great encyclical, *Populorum Progressio* (On the Development of Peoples), it is a desire we have been challenged healthily to foster. Since self-fulfillment, relentlessly pursued, can produce egotistical monsters, committed solely to the satisfaction and gratification of their own instinctual, social, or even religious needs, it is crucial that the acceptable means to this necessary goal of fulfillment be clearly grasped and integrated into life.

The striving for personal fulfillment is a sign of the times, and has attracted the syntheses and insights of many writers and spiritual directors. No one among the classical spiritual writers has more to say on this topic than the Carmelite reformer, John of the Cross. Unfortunately, many people's initial encounters with his life and thought have been negative. Others, unaware of the need for a historical-critical analysis of his work, have become spiritual fundamentalists in their interpretation of his teaching. Even the uninterested

know of his call to sacrifice, and to live through the pain and darkness of the "nights." John is frequently identified with denial, not
fulfillment; the lonely ascent of Mount Carmel, not growth with others; the deliberate choice of that which is most difficult, not that
which leads directly to enrichment. In short, at first glance, John
does not seem the best guide to human enrichment and growth.
However, John of the Cross is not only a figure of prime importance
in Christian spirituality, but also one of the most well-rounded and
integrated personalities of history. He is undoubtedly one of the few
really great success stories from the perspective of human growth
and personal fulfillment.

In the last half century, Christians in greater numbers than
ever before have sought from John the answers to their needs. Unfortunately, this most often results in a "self-service cafeteria" approach, where pseudo-disciples of John have found appropriate sayings and captions for books of photography, or slogans for their
banners, and even support in a minor "night." I hardly think John
would be interested in any of these, even the last. Rather, he would
seek from us what he sought from followers in his day: a total
singleminded commitment to the whole journey of faith and love.
The end of the journey is twofold: union with God and complete
transformation and rediscovery of self. John's life and system are not
only examples of our awesome call to union with God, but also of
humanity's call to the genuine rediscovery of self and personal fulfillment. Though we seek union, and experience personal fulfillment as a byproduct, the latter is nevertheless an essential of his
spiritual system. Without denying the primacy of the union with
God, it is the human fulfillment that we consider in this section.

John was twenty-five years old when Teresa of Avila asked him
to cooperate in the reform of the male branch of Carmel. By the age
of thirty-five he had also studied extensively, done a lot of formation
work, been spiritual director to many, and yet given himself so much
to the search for God that it is generally thought that his mystical
experience was already mature at this time. He was a busy administrator, a reformer, and a writer, all time-consuming tasks. He had
also spent many months in prison, due to conflicts of jurisdiction
between the old and the new branches of Carmel. Yet his busy and
potentially anxious life never turned him aside from his search for

God. He always gave the impression of being a unified and integrated person. Long before he met Teresa, he had already learned some of the greatest lessons of the spiritual life.

John went in search of God and was willing to pay the price. In his own journey of faith and love he was so committed to the double goal of union with God and self-fulfillment that he gave up all immediate satisfactions in order that he could gain everything in God. The "nothing" (*nada*) of the nights' denials was a means to the "everything" (*todo*) of the union and self-fulfillment. One of John's most distinctive characteristics was the ability to deny himself through love and desire for his goal. In the *Canticle*, he expresses his conviction: "The soul who does not know how to lose herself does not find herself" (C, 29, 11). In the same section he says: "The one who walks in the love of God seeks neither gain nor reward, but seeks only to lose with the will all things and self for God; and this loss the lover judges to be a gain." John's experience had shown him that denying the faculties their immediate satisfaction was not really a loss, but a means to a state of union and life-enrichment that ought to be the goal of anyone interested in the rediscovery of authentic self. So John could say: "Even if human beings do not free their heart of joy in temporal goods for the sake of God and the demands of Christian perfection, they ought to do so because of the resulting temporal advantages, prescinding from the spiritual ones.... [They] acquire the virtue of liberality.... Moreover, they acquire liberty of spirit, clarity of reason, rest, tranquility, peaceful confidence in God.... They obtain more joy and recreation in creatures.... In detachment from things they acquire a clearer knowledge of them" (A, 3, 20, 2).

John himself was the embodiment of these satisfying effects of the journey of faith, as can be seen in the exceptional beauty of his poetry and prose, his perceptiveness in spiritual direction, his warmth and affection in dealing with others, his clear understanding of divine things, his empathy for fellow pilgrims, and in the peace and resignation of his last months.

More important than these byproducts was the thrill of union with God described so delightfully by John (C, 36, 5; 11, 10). It was obviously an experience he never forgot. John's short life shows humanity its great potential for union with God. He also shows us

that when he gave himself unwaveringly to God he became a new
person, one of the most wholesome and integrated personalities of
history.

John's Understanding of the Human Condition

Mystics are witnesses to God. We look to them for some small
but significant insight that helps us catch a new glimpse of God.
Generally, we turn to anthropologists, psychologists, sociologists,
and social scientists to help us understand human nature, its condition and development. However, for believers, the mystic is a source
not only for knowledge of God, but also for knowledge of humanity, because whenever a mystic talks about God, the human person
is always central to the issue. God's self-revelation is communicated
to men and women, in their history. It is precisely when we contrast
the two—human nature and God—that we see human persons most
clearly, in their weakness and helplessness, but also in their call to
glory and union. Thus, the mystic can give us great insight into humanity.

John deals extensively with the human condition, maintaining
a focus on the person throughout the journey to God.[61] He shows
considerable empathy for the person in need of transformation.
Presenting a clearly defined system, with established stages of
growth and recognizable characteristics of each stage, John nevertheless is very attentive to an individual's situation and subjective
reactions. John's introduction to the *Ascent* stresses that it is concern
for struggling individuals that impels him to write his book, to remove the ignorance of some and the misguidance others have received from their directors. Moreover, although John starts his work
with the night of sense and the call to active purification from the
attachments to sense objects, he also accepts the fact that some
people can be spiritually helped by such objects. "The will, then,
does not have to avoid such experiences when they produce this
devotion and prayer, but it can profit by them, and even ought to
for the sake of so holy an exercise" (A, 3, 24, 4). Moreover, John
treats each person's condition as unique, and avoids any rigid uni-
formity in the application of his system. "Although individuals may

have truly reached union, this union will be proportioned to their lesser or greater capacity, for not all souls attain an identical degree of union. This depends on what the Lord wishes to grant each one" (A, 2, 5, 10).

John shows considerable empathy toward struggling people, and his evaluation of them is basically positive.[62] On the other hand his description of the human condition sounds very negative and could easily discourage readers. He speaks of "the harm, privative as well as positive, that appetites engender in the soul," considering that they "weary, torment, darken, defile, and weaken" individuals, making them lukewarm in the practice of virtue (A, 1, 6–10). When he speaks of the harm caused by seeking one's joy in temporal goods, he states that this false joy leads to withdrawal from God, underestimation of the seriousness of one's false affection, complete abandonment of God, and forgetfulness of the saving God as one makes a god of temporal attachments (A, 3, 19). His lists of defects in beginners (N, 1, 2) and in proficients (N, 2, 2) leave readers wondering how these individuals can possibly turn their situations around. But John is not a pessimist, nor does he despise humanity; rather, he objectively describes the human condition, portraying the starting point in very negative terms, perhaps more negative than other writers use, but then presents a potential renewal and transformation of personality far more enriching than other writers suggest. Beginning lower, and ending higher, for John the journey is longer and the vocation greater. John sees a great distance between the beginning and the end of the journey, but this is a challenging opportunity for growth. Thus, although his initial description of the human condition is very negative, John still affirms that the person is essentially good, and claims that "the disordered soul possesses in its natural being the perfection that God bestowed when creating it" (A, 1, 9, 3). Although some mystical systems run the risk of being interpreted pantheistically, John's does not. At the end of the journey, when we are transformed in the union with God, we nevertheless retain our humanity and are not absorbed in God. "When God grants this supernatural favor to the soul, so great a union is caused that all the things of both God and the soul become one in participant transformation, and the soul appears to be God more than a soul. Indeed, it is God by participation. Yet truly, its being…is naturally as distinct from God's as it was before" (A, 2, 5, 7).

John accepts the traditional divisions of a person into body and soul, with five external senses, two internal senses (phantasy and imagination), three internal spiritual faculties (intellect, memory, and will), and four passions (joy, sorrow, hope, and fear). Although the many divisions can seem complicated, John's underlying conviction is that any one of these can have a profound influence on the whole human person, and thus each one must be purified and redirected to God.

John does not view the person statically but dynamically. The traditional approach views the human person as divided into two parts: the lower, made up of senses and instincts, is what we have in common with animals; the higher part comprises the spiritual faculties. This division easily led to the false conclusion that the work of the higher faculties was somehow automatically more "spiritual" than activity with the lower senses and appetites, and that commitment to religious matters was always better than commitment to matters related to the senses. John views the person dynamically, with all the faculties, "higher" and "lower," united in the integral dedication to God of one's whole personality. As often happens when a new insight is attained, John still uses the received vocabulary (A, 3, 26, 3). However, John's dynamic understanding sees the *whole* person directing every aspect of life to God. This he refers to as the *spiritual* person, but to avoid divisive vocabulary, we can speak of the *God-directed* person. Whether such a person is involved in liturgy, prayer, spiritual direction, community, use of money, sexual activity, or eating and drinking, all is directed to God.[63] The sensory or sensual person is the one who seeks self-satisfaction and self-gratification, whether involved in eating and drinking, sexual activity, use of money, community, spiritual direction, prayer, or liturgy. This self-centered person turns everything to selfish satisfaction. John's insight has many significant consequences, showing the positive values of God-directed lives in those who may be married, or spend their lives in community-building, or any temporal sphere of life. It also highlights the possibility of becoming overly attached to aspects of religion, using them for comfort or security. After all, the varied spheres of life are all God's gifts, and can all be used well or abused. The ascetical battle is for the conquest of the whole person, making every aspect of life part of one's integral dedication to God. Problems in the post-Vatican II Church have often revolved around our attachments to religious objects (e.g., altar rails, statues), religious habits, religious power, external formulations of doctrine, liturgical rituals, or religious offices. Contemporary religious divisiveness and polarization tends to center on particular religious issues that rarely concern essentials and frequently have to do with externals. Attachment to religious things is often defended as devotion, fidelity, and orthodoxy, but can equally represent the self-seeking of one who finds gratification in this kind of control and satisfaction. In John's Sketch of the Mount, the two broad (and, we have noted, dead-end) valleys that people mistakenly think lead to the summit are earthly and heavenly goods; both are thought to lead to union with God, but do not. Religious attachments show human weakness as much as any other attachment. In reading John's challenging message, we should not interpret statically what he intends to be viewed dynamically, nor apply to a part of the person what John sees as a way of viewing the whole.

Starting Point: A Disordered Situation

John is convinced that many are called to union, and he is saddened that so many do not succeed in attaining their goal. Disorder is measured in relation to what ought to be, and appreciating the call to union and renewal contrasts with the pitiable state of those who fail to respond to the invitation. John is appalled by the disorder in which men and women find themselves.

John's consideration of the human person is practical and functional, insofar as his own goal is not merely to understand but to change people. He sees individuals at the outset of the spiritual journey as being in a completely raw state, with no initial hierarchy of values to guide them. They ought to follow the gradual and progressive subordination of themselves to the life of the Spirit, thus establishing God-directed lives. Unfortunately, this rarely happens.

Rather, individuals naturally drift toward a life dominated by the search for sensory pleasure. For John, the individual's task is to stop this process, purifying the false values by redirecting one's life toward God. Few people are willing to endure the hardships of the rigorous process of purification, and so most end up drifting toward self-satisfaction.

The disordered situation that results from false attachments is a serious hindrance to any further growth.[64] It hides a person's true image, dignity, and potential, as John details in his comments on the harm incurred by finding our joy in sensory, moral, or religious goods, instead of exclusively in God (N, 1, 6–10). The resulting disorder can only be remedied by the "night."

As we have seen elsewhere, John understands that the desires or appetites constantly influence the faculties, moving them toward or away from objects.[65] When these desires are not properly directed toward God, the disordered situation, whatever appetite is the cause, imposes a process of continual regression. Thus John says that "spiritual persons must exercise great care that in their heart and joy they do not become attached to temporal goods. They must fear lest, through a gradual increase, their small attachments become great" (A, 3, 20, 1).

Besides the continual backsliding and loss of dignity it causes, the disordered situation in which individuals find themselves also blocks both God's action in their lives and the discovery of their own potential. Although capable of union with God, individuals are stunted by attachment to, and affection for, objects that are not part of a God-directed life. "Any little thing that adheres to them in this life is sufficient to so burden and bewitch them that they do not perceive the harm or note the lack of their immense goods, or know their own capacity" (F, 3, 18). Disorder can be caused even by a small attachment that provokes an undesirable refocusing of one's values. "It is an amazing thing that the least of these goods is enough so to encumber these faculties, capable of infinite goods, that they cannot receive these infinite goods until they are completely empty" (*ibid.*).

Disordered appetites are the characteristic of disordered men and women, individuals who have not learned self-control, or have

consistently let themselves be guided by the search for sensory pleasure, or are unwilling to accept the sacrifices of journeying along the
narrow path. Sometimes the consequent regression occurs without
a person realizing it, as if it just happened spontaneously. However,
according to John the harmful effects clearly show that one's approach to spiritual growth is not good and needs serious adjust-
ment, even a new foundation altogether. Some individuals, with all
the good will in the world, remain paralyzed in their disorder, without understanding why. John's response is firm; the system upon
which their lives are based is wrong, and must be replaced by the
systematic purification of every appetite, and the deliberate redirection of each to God. "People, indeed, are ignorant who think it is
possible to reach this high state of union with God without first
emptying their appetite of all the natural and supernatural things
that can be hindrance to them" (A, 1, 5, 2).

The disorders that concern John are not the failures or imperfections into which a just person falls each day. Rather, the disorders here are profound misdirections of life that affect the core of
our lives and value system. Sometimes the disorder is difficult to
discover because it is made to appear quite normal, justified as an
acceptable practice in a particular culture, rooted in the people's
common life, and even religiously supported; when this happens,
we see the seriousness of the disorder. In fact, the major disorders
of the spiritual life need careful discernment, just as vocations or
common mission do. "And even if the spirit is unaware of any harm,
distraction is at least secretly caused" (A, 3, 22, 2). The rooted disorders of a culture destroy it from within, as "the offspring of vipers
are said to do within the mother: While growing within her they eat
away at her entrails and finally kill her, remaining alive at her ex-
pense" (A, 1, 10, 3).

From our earlier reflections on John, we can already appreciate that his solution to the disorder is the purification of each desire or appetite, until every dimension of the person is integrated in
a unified dedication to the Lord. For John, to conquer the appetites
is really to use them in freedom. In reading John we must always
keep an eye on the present situation in our own lives, society, and
the church. What are the major factors causing our situation of disorder? Probably we received them from a previous generation, and

will pass on our failures, rooted in the culture, to the next generation. We have received disordered attitudes to the poor and to
women, and we still live them out, at times sacrilegiously justifying
our injustices, as our predecessors did with slavery. Unfortunately,
we too may be passing on to the next generation as much rational-
ized sin as we received. Sexism is still present in society and church,
falsely justified and sacrilegiously supported. The extensive attachment to particular "theologies" that are sometimes little more than
ideologies continues to maintain power and control as the chief
motivating factors for many who pursue their own careers under the
guise of service. Disregard of the poor and oppressed increases, institutionalized in national legislation, and people seem to prefer
instruments of hate and war to the alleviation of the hardships of
the less fortunate. Abuse of drugs, money, sex, and power is so per-
vasive that it has become the normal order of the day, influencing
the whole of society, both civil and sometimes even ecclesiastical.
Significant growth in prayer is hardly possible in those who ignore,
oppress, or abuse others, who glorify their own position and seek to
crush all opposition in the name of religion. The church as a community and in its individual members cries out for healing, but this
will require consistent dedication to the systematic purifications of
the night. No doubt in time some will accept the call, but others find
so much self-satisfaction in their chosen course that they will hardly
let it go.

Quest for Authenticity

John never speaks disparagingly of human nature; rather, he
always sees human nature as a gift from God, with great potential.
Basically, the journeys of active and passive purification will develop
the good in us, or else the refusal to be committed to the narrow
path of the ascent will cause our potential for evil to flourish. There
is no middle ground in this quest for authentic growth. The journey to God, with its purification of sense, and its purification and
redirection of the intellect, memory, and will (in faith, hope, and
love, respectively) is a preparation for union, and is at the same time
a discovery of the person's true and authentic self.

John believes we ought to have a God-directed life, but left to ourselves we drift toward a self-directed life. Our inauthentic self must be refocused to good, first by stopping the drive towards self-satisfaction and then by cleaning away the false attachments. "A bird caught in birdlime has a twofold task: It must free itself and cleanse itself. And by satisfying their appetites, people suffer in a twofold way: They must detach themselves and, after being detached, clean themselves of what has clung to them" (Sayings, 22).

One might well paint over a dirty wall in a house, but would hardly do the same to the dirty walls of a gothic cathedral. In the latter case sandblasting is needed in order to uncover the prior beauty of the stone and discover a masterpiece. For John, our authentic self is found by removing the encrustations of false attachments and scraping away the accumulations of absolutized possession. After all, people are not the sum of their possessions, whether material, religious, moral, or spiritual. Rather, each one is potentially a perfect masterpiece from the Creator's hand. The challenge of the active nights is to strip away from ourselves what is really not us, and to get rid of those possessions which sap our singleminded commitment to God. The authentic self is not made rich by possessing, but certainly becomes rich through the poverty of detachment. In the earlier sections of the *Canticle* John states: "This is how we recognize persons who truly love God: if they are content with nothing less than God. But what am I saying, if they are content? Even if they possess everything they will not be content; in fact the more they have, the less satisfied they will be. Satisfaction of heart is not found is the possession of things, but in being stripped of them all and in poverty of spirit" (C, 1, 14).

John considers persons inauthentic who merely accumulate goods, believing that the more they have the better they are. People discover their authentic selves when they completely empty themselves so that they can be filled with God, and thus realize their greatest potential. All values in the world are worth nothing when compared with the infinite goodness of God. "Compared to the infinite goodness of God, all the goodness of the creatures of the world can be called wickedness. Nothing is good save God only [Lk 18:19]. Those who set their hearts on the good things of the world becomes extemely wicked in the sight of God" (A, 1, 4, 4).

Individuals who appreciate their call to be filled with God acknowledge that the best goal is to be empty. Thus, the journey to God is one of becoming poor and stripping oneself of false attachments. This poverty and nakedness must be attained on all levels, not only material, but moral, spiritual, and religious as well. "Let them know what you profess, which is the naked Christ.... For the poor in spirit are happier and more constant in the midst of want because they have placed their all in nothingness, and in all things they thus find freedom of heart" (Letter 16).

A significant obstacle to reaching this authenticity is spiritual avarice, when people "hardly ever seem content with the spirit God gives them. They become unhappy and peevish because they don't find the consolation they want in spiritual things" (N 1, 3, 1). The quest for authenticity means a total emptying of self, letting go even of those religious experiences that calm, console, and comfort us. "People who are truly devout direct their devotion mainly to the invisible object represented.... Even when the motives and means that bring the soul closer to God are taken from them, they remain calm" (A, 3, 35, 5).

Personal authenticity does not come spontaneously, but requires deliberate redirecting of all dimensions of personality; external social conventions, instinctual tendencies, and all appetites that affect the root of who we are. Religion will always remain merely one sector of life, and everything will remain superficial, unless we arrive at the core of our being. Then, completely empty and aware of our own poverty and nakedness, we find God. "If individuals would eliminate these impediments and veils and live in pure nakedness and poverty of spirit, ...their soul in its simplicity and purity would then be immediately tranformed into simple and pure Wisdom, the Son of God" (A, 2, 15, 4).

As we are drawn by God through the night of sense, gifted with the full and joy-filled life on the plateau between the valleys of the nights, and later drawn through the decisive period of the passive night of spirit, the journey in faith and love is itself precisely the journey of poverty and nakedness, when we abandon all that does not strengthen true love or prepare us for union and the rediscovery of our true gifted self.

John never attacks or criticizes natural activities. Objects are not viewed as negative in themselves, but only in the possessiveness with which we deal with them. Thus, the purpose of John's system is not destruction, but the acquisition of true values. Poverty and nakedness leave us not with nothing but with everything. Rather than destroying any human power, John is urging us to let each faculty find its true value and achieve its greatest function. The authentic self is found within the depths of each person, where there is the wonderful potential for transformation in God. "To love is to labor to divest and deprive oneself for God of all that is not God. When this is done the soul will be illumined by and transformed in God" (A, 2, 5, 7).

John's challenge to become poor and to strip oneself naked has made him unpopular, since it makes him seem to be against the material world, and even dualistic. However, John's quest for authenticity resonates with the hopes of modern men and women. Moreover, he seeks to remove "all that is not God," and to choose only God and the things of God. The purity of his vision and the courageous singlemindedness with which he pursues it also are appreciated today. Following the Vatican Council's affirmation of the goodness and autonomy of earthly realities, even John's poverty and nakedness, understood as a call to integration, can also be appreciated as a valued part of his message.

Integral Human Renewal

Union with God implies a profound fulfillment of human potential.[66] Both union and renewal of personality go together, in John's vision. Each of us is truly capable of God, and can never be satisfied unless we are filled with God. "The soul's center is God. When it has reached God with all the capacity of its being and the strength of its operation and inclination, it will have attained its final and deepest center in God" (F, 1, 12). Having previously emptied oneself, an individual receives enjoyment and delight when filled with God (F, 3, 18). Moreover, even when describing the resulting transformation, John avoids the pantheistic overtones that some other mystics slip into. There is no *absorption* but rather a wonderful *transformation* of the human person, involving human fulfillment (A, 1, 9, 3). In this union, the person receives "fortitude, wisdom, love, beauty, grace, and goodness, and so on. Because God is all these things, a person enjoys them in only one touch of God, and the soul rejoices within its faculties and within its substance" (F, 2, 21).

Besides this experience of union, then, we also find that commitment to the purifications of the journey leads to profound enrichment. The many "nothings" (*nadas*) lead to "everything" (*todo*), even on a human level. Control of faculties and appetites leads to spiritual freedom and real joy in the life of the Spirit. "Oh, what a sheer grace it is for the soul to be freed from the house of its senses.... [Such persons] will understand how the life of the spirit is true freedom and wealth and embodies inestimable goods" (N, 2, 14, 3). It produces "clarity of reason, rest, tranquility, peaceful confidence in God, and in their will, the true cult and homage of God" (A, 3, 20, 2). John also claims that only the person who is not possessive toward a particular object can truly enjoy it and find a God-directed satisfaction in it. "Those, then, whose joy is unpossessive of things rejoice in them all as though they possessed them all" (A, 3, 20, 3). Anxiety and the cares of life decrease and distractions in prayer cease (*ibid.*). A further result is the gift of clear judgment and the ability to evaluate clearly what influences our lives.

Even our human senses are refined and can be exercised with new force in what is now a totally God-directed life. The person who has made the journey rediscovers true joy and satisfaction in the creatures he or she had "abandoned." "They obtain more joy and recreation in creatures through the dispossession of them" (A, 3, 20, 2). Further benefits include intensified satisfaction in the use of the senses and an increased sensitivity toward their natural objects. "The person whose sense is purged of sensible objects and ordered to reason procures from the first movements the delight of savory contemplation and awareness of God" (A, 3, 26, 5). John even claims that the senses, when purified of false attachments, develop an ability to react to the joys of the Spirit. "It can...through a certain spiritual overflow, receive sensible refreshment and delight from them. This delight attracts the corporal senses" (C, 40, 6).

John does not hesitate to speak of the benefits to the body of union with God. He speaks of a "feeling of great delight and glory, even in the outermost joints of the hands and feet" (F, 2, 22). This thrilling feeling of health and wellbeing is part of the human fulfillment that comes with the commitment to which John calls us.

John also speaks of the purified person's ability to penetrate and know "the inclinations and talents of other persons and what lies in the heart or interior spirit," as well as "the thoughts of others or their interior state" (A, 2, 26, 14). He claims that this ability is specifically the result of the increased acuteness of the senses, i.e., an ability to pick up on even the smallest sensory cues.

Along with these signs of renewal, those who journey to the summit and discover their authentic selves within also discover a new dimension of themselves, a zone naturally divine. This discovery of God at the center of one's being results from the work of purification. "As soon as natural things are driven out of the enamored soul, the divine are naturally and supernaturally infused" (A, 2, 15, 4). In this discovery, "love is the soul's inclination, strength, and power in making its way to God, for love unites it with God. The more degrees of love it has, the more deeply it enters into God and centers itself in him" (F, 1, 13). This union in love brings profound peace, and through this encounter, "which is the Holy Spirit's visit of love, the Bridegroom, the Son of God, is himself sublimely communicated" (C, 17, 8).

This union, which is "more wonderful than all that can be said of it" (C, 31, 2), produces this personal renewal that includes liberty of spirit, recovery of sense, and openness to God's activity within one's heart.

Personal fulfillment is never sought after directly, but is a byproduct. To come to union with God we must uproot all attachments, whether individual or collective, and make God and divine interests the only focal point of life. All else must be integrated into this, or it will sap the strength of our commitment. If we can actively provoke and passively accept the purifications of the nights, God may draw us to divine life. Though effort is necessary on our part, we will later look back to acknowledge that we were never really the ones journeying to God, but that God was always journeying toward us, drawing us to divine life. With God will be given the thrill of union and a qualitative modification of human life.

Although John is concerned with the move to union, he also manifests and documents his convictions on the human fulfillment that is a result of these journeys. John's vision is biblical, a vision of an exodus from slavery to the enrichment of the promised land. Few mystics state as clearly as John that the union sought is profoundly enriching on every level of personality.

CHAPTER SIX

The Living and True God in the System of John of the Cross

Searching for God

No issue is more important to humanity than the existence and nature of God. Those who claim a special experience of God are viewed as holy and the place of encounter sacred. Founders of religions have often institutionalized their experiences, and the special knowledge they received. Followers then call such founders the enlightened one (Buddha), the conqueror (Jaina), the great father (Abraham), the great teacher (Lao Tzu), or simply great one (Mahavira). All humanity, from primitive times up to the present, searches for God.

A small number of religions are also based on revelations, insisting that God has come in search of humanity, like "the hound of heaven." Among these revealed religions is Christianity, which also insists that God has sent his only Son to share life with humankind. Mystics have a particular interest in God and claim that their personal revelatory experience somehow shares in and confirms the foundational revelation. John of the Cross stands out even among the mystics, because of the purity of his message, his relentless pursuit of God, and the clarity of his descriptions of the nature of the encounter with God.

John's focus is on the Trinity, as we see in the "Romances" and the *Canticle* and *Living Flame*. "The soul proclaims how the three Persons of the Most Blessed Trinity, the Father, the Son, and the

Holy Spirit, are the ones who effect this divine work of union in it"
(F, 2, 1). However, when John speaks of God, it is always with a concentration on the effects the Trinity produces in the human
person's deepest center: the "delightful wound" attributed to the
Holy Spirit, the "taste of eternal life" attributed to the Son, and the
"transformation, a gift by which all debts are fully paid," attributed
to the gentle hand of the Father (F, 2, 1). So whenever John talks
about the Trinity, he focuses on interactions between humanity and
the Trinity—the actions of individuals, yearning for God, or the
actions of God, drawing people to divine life.

John's approach resonates with modern people's values, since
he is so determined and consistent in his pursuit of God, so
singleminded in his relationship of choice-oriented love for God, so
articulate in presenting his profound experience of God, and so
contemporary in his universal call to quality spiritual commitment.

Although mystics may claim to tell us something special about
God, they generally end by describing ways of *encountering* God.
Readers then run the danger of confusing the believer's activities in
searching for God with the essence of God. "All the knowledge of
God possible in this life, however extensive it may be, is inadequate,
for it is only partial knowledge and very remote" (C, 6, 5). Most
mystics help by giving us details of their search for God. Moreover,
the God they describe is the God of faith. "Faith…gives and communicates God himself, but covered with the silver of faith. Yet it
does not for this reason fail to give him to us truly" (C, 12, 4). In this
life it is impossible to see God as one does in the next life, but faith
reveals the secrets that await us. "The substance of the secrets is God
himself, for God is the substance and concept of faith, and faith is
the secret and the mystery" (C, 1, 10). Loving faith is the means of
union with God as we journey to the summit of Mount Carmel, and
the deeper our faith, the deeper our potential for union. "For the
likeness between faith and God is so close that no other difference
exists than that between believing in God and seeing him…. The
greater one's faith, the closer is one's union with God" (A, 2, 9, 1).
Like other mystics, John emphasizes the journey to God more than
the end.[67] We get to know God in our experience of the search. This
search involves a journey of faith and a journey of love. John describes the former in the diptych of the *Ascent of Mount Carmel* and

the *Dark Night of the Soul.* The imagery is of climbing, darkness, and night. John describes the latter journey of love in the *Spiritual Canticle* and *Living Flame of Love,* where the symbolism is matrimonial.

These two ways to God are complementary and both are necessary. As an individual journeys to God, "truths are infused by faith" (C, 12, 6), even though they are barely sketched rather than presented clearly in detail. "Over this sketch of faith, the sketch of love is drawn in the will of the lover" (C, 12, 7).

Journey of Faith

John describes the journey along the narrow path to the summit of Mount Carmel as a journey of faith (N, Prologue). This journey consists of the purifications and illuminations of the nights. Thus, the journey is a dark night. "Now this road is faith, and for the intellect faith is also like a dark night" (A, 1, 2, 1). This night of faith involves the gradual purification of all false images of God, as the intellect is emptied of all false and partial understandings of God and is supported by faith alone. "To be prepared for this divine union the intellect must be cleansed and emptied of everything relating to sense, divested and liberated of everything clearly intelligible, inwardly pacified and silenced, and supported by faith alone" (A, 2, 9, 1).

The nakedness and poverty of spirit gradually purify all accumulated false images of God. "Poor, abandoned, and unsupported by any of the apprehensions of my soul, ...left to darkness in pure faith, which is a dark night, ...I went out from my low manner of understanding, and my feeble way of loving, and my poor and limited method of finding satisfaction in God" (N, 2, 4, 1). Those who do not purify their faith remain stunted in their knowledge of God. Some do not want to undergo this purification, because their image of God is part of the comfort and consolation they find in religion. Such attachment is unfortunate and leads people to accept gods of their own creation. Such people even project their own image onto the divine when they look at God and divine realities. In fact, some who would like to encounter God do not, because they remain blocked by their own pleasant image of God, acquired over many

years. Such an image, no matter how sublime, is an idol, and these
persons end up adoring a god of the own creation. John says that it
is as if such people have a cataract shrouding the eye of judgment.
They cannot see clearly because their false or incomplete images of
God block their vision. He concludes: "One will infallibly come to
consider the things of God as not of God, and the things that are
not of God as of God" (F, 3, 73).

John does not allow anything to block his search for union
with God. Not only can we be blocked by sensuality, attachment to
money and politics, and so on, but also by our own pious images of
God from prayer, retreats, or liturgy. Images can be helpful, but they
are only signposts to God, and even the most wonderful is still a creature, a potential idol that must not be clung to as we get to know
God better. "The most that can be felt and tasted of God in this life
is infinitely distant from God and the pure possession of him" (A, 2,
4, 4). Those who drag along behind them images of God exclusively
from past experiences end up imprisoned by their own past every
time they think of God. The denial and conquest of human limita-
tions in knowing and loving God is achieved by following the way of
faith, in two stages or rhythms: a conceptual rhythm and a vital
rhythm.

The elimination of false or inadequate images of God is part
of a conceptual rhythm, a rhythm of knowing/unknowing that purifies all our preconceptions about God in the journey of faith. "If
the soul in traveling this road leans on any elements of its own
knowledge or of its experience or knowledge of God, it will easily
go astray" (A, 2, 4, 3). Rather, the individual learns to abide in the
darkness of faith, which is its only guide. "However impressive may
be one's knowledge or experience of God, that knowledge or experience will have no resemblance to God and amount to very little"
(*ibid.*).

Thus, the conceptual rhythm in the journey of faith goes beyond all images, concluding that God is not like any creature. This
is the work of the active nights and is explained in the *Ascent*. Convinced that all human ability to understand God is foolishness when
compared to God, believers are called to "set aside their own knowledge and walk in God's service like unlearned children"; they must

"advance to union with God's wisdom by unknowing rather than by knowing" (A, 1, 4, 5). Thus, the journey of the dark night of faith helps us appreciate that God is not like creatures.

John offers a detailed program to purify and rectify our understanding of God, regarding both the content of faith (A, 2, 2–3) and our own attitudes to believing (A, 2, 4).[68] Faith is the personal acceptance of God's gratuitous blessing, and includes belief in the transcendence of God—not confining God but letting God be who God wishes to be. While unruly appetites may be dangers to faith, the principal dangers are supernatural (A, 2, 10). John focuses on all our cognitive capacities, all possible ways of gaining knowledge of faith's object, including the external senses, internal senses, and intellect. All must be purified and left empty to be filled by God.

The vital rhythm, the rhythm of living, is a more painful part of the journey of faith than the conceptual rhythm. It is a passive experience, detailed in the *Dark Night,* and leads believers to appreciate that God does not entirely correspond to our ideas about the divine, nor does God act in the way we expect. It purifies our images of God vitally, as we experience God acting toward us in ways we never thought possible. This passive illumination makes us feel impure, weak, and wretched in comparison with God. Individuals may feel that God has rejected them, that they are unworthy of God and will never be worthy again (N, 2, 5, 5). The intense suffering convinces such individuals that God has rejected them and cast them into darkness (N, 2, 6, 2). It is a struggle to understand why God does not act with the forgiveness, compassion, and love they have come to expect. Describing how such a soul feels, John says, "it feels very vividly indeed the shadow of death, the sighs of death, and the sorrows of hell, all of which reflect the feeling of God's absence, of being chastised and rejected by him, and of being unworthy of him, as well as the object of his anger" (N 2, 6, 2).

In these two stages of the journey of faith God shows seekers that none of their ideas correspond exactly to God, and that God is never captured by our concepts. They are challenged to abandon their previous knowledge and awareness and dedicate themselves confidently and serenely to a divine reality they do not understand.[69] After all ideas of God collapse, as the idols they are, God remains.

We are not left empty, but approach a clearer understanding of divine transcendence. When Doña Juana de Pedraza experienced similar abandonment and emptiness, John assured her: "You were never better off than now because you were never so humble or so submissive, ...nor did you serve God so purely and so disinterestedly as now" (Letter 19).[70] The realism of John's own faith is his acknowledgment that although God *seems* distant, God never really *is* distant. Later we may put things into perspective and recognize that it is we ourselves who are distant from God, but at the time this is not how it is experienced. As difficulties arise in this anxious time, John recommends that seekers center all their questions on Christ, the Word of God. "In giving us his Son, his only Word, (for he possesses no other), he spoke everything to us at once in this sole Word—and he has no more to say" (A, 2, 22, 3). This revelation is the object of our faith and authenticates all other experiences. All faith and all God has to give us is synthesized in Jesus, in whom we now encounter the divine will.

Other religions besides Christianity acknowledge an experience of darkness and faith. However, the principal agent in the Christian's spiritual journey is *God* who is drawing the individual toward divine life. It is not a journey of a lonely individual, who becomes caught and possibly lost in an experience of absolute dread. Since the Christian is being drawn toward God, and now and again catches sight of the loving Lord who may seem distant but is active in the journey, there is never a total dread or despairing abandonment. The journey of faith is difficult but will also be complemented by love, as we shall see.

Today many people appreciate John's teaching on journeying to God in faith. It is a journey that many contemporaries feel called to make. Changes that previously occurred over a generation now take only a few years or less. More theologians, actively reflecting on the knowledge of God, are alive today than at any other time in Christian history. Spiritual leaders, with their recommendations for spiritual growth and prayer development, are also found in larger numbers than ever. Challenges to reinterpret our images and understanding of God come more frequently and easily than ever before, and many individuals find themselves in the early stages of the purifying journey of faith. However, the journey of faith is no longer reserved to individuals. Ecclesial groups, the church as a whole, social groups, and humanity too, find themselves called to purify images, to be open to the future and ready to reintegrate their vision of life under God.

Journey of Love

Many believers know of John's way of faith through the dark night, but often pass over his more important way of love. In fact, John sees the two as closely linked, since faith is initiated and maintained by love. "The soul, then, states that 'fired with love's urgent longings' it passed through this night of sense to union with the Beloved" (A, 1, 14, 2). Speaking of the passive night, John focuses again on love, challenging a person who seeks union to "make room in the spirit for the enkindling and burning of the love that this dark and secret contemplation bears and communicates to the soul" (N, 1, 10, 6).

As we have repeatedly noted, John's journey of faith, with its purification of all false images of God, is not a way of increased conceptual knowledge, through which individuals study the nature of God and progressively clarify the notion of divinity. Many individuals are attracted by this intellectual exercise that satisfies their need to possess God and brings the transcendent into their grasp. Clearly this is not John's focus, since the way of conceptual knowledge ends with images and ideas that need purification. The journey of faith includes a confident loving self-gift that substitutes for the light lost in the darkness of the struggle. "Although the soul in her progress does not have the support of any particular interior light of the intellect, or of any exterior guide..., love alone, which at this period burns by soliciting the heart for the Beloved, is what guides and moves her" (N, 2, 25, 4). Through all purifications that are part of the night, an individual is sustained by a sense of love. "In the midst of these dark and loving afflictions, the soul feels a certain companionship," so that "when this weight of anxious darkness passes, it often feels alone" (N, 2, 11, 7).

So, love is an intimate part of the journey of faith. In addition, John speaks of the journey to God as a way of love:

I went out calling you, but you were gone.
. . . .
If by chance you see
him I love most,
tell him I am sick, I suffer, and I die.

Seeking my Love
I will head for the mountains and for watersides.... (C, 1–3)

The *Canticle* is filled with the imagery of love, and the *Living Flame* begins and ends with the same focus: "O living flame of love...how tenderly you swell my heart with love!"

The way of love, as found in some mystics, gives rise to criticisms that their approaches are merely expressions or sublimations of their own need for physical or sexual intimacy, but this is not the case with John. His way of love is a rich, mature, total self-gift. The search, encounter, union, and mutual possession are achieved through choice-oriented decisions that imply painful renunciations that shape the personality of the searcher. John advises anyone who longs for union with God to "seek him in faith and love, without desiring to find satisfaction in anything, or delight, or desiring to understand anything other than what you ought to know. Faith and love are like the blind person's guides" (C, 1, 11).

The purification of desire in the way of love is a long process that must be handled carefully, lest our affectivity be divided among many objects. John seeks the integration of the affective life, so that love is united and focused on God alone.[71] Those who have many desires and affections disperse the strength of their wills, and can no longer love God alone. "Because the force of the desire is divided, the appetite becomes weaker than if it were completely fixed on one object" (A, 1, 10, 1). Although John distinguishes the sensitive and spiritual objects of knowledge in the *Ascent,* the schema he uses in book three for discussing the purification of love and will cuts across such distinctions. He seeks a unity of the affective life, integrally focused on God.

One must purify love by controlling one's desires for satisfaction in attractive but potentially encumbering external goods, whether temporal, natural, or sensible—even more so in the case of religious values, including the moral, supernatural, and spiritual.

The latter can be particularly deceptive when linked to justifying reasons, criteria, and convictions. Individuals can dedicate themselves to religious causes that are often nothing more than collective appetites, weakening Christian love. Thus, we have witnessed in recent years the increase in divisive and loveless factions in the church, under the disguise of fidelity to tradition or "the spirit of Vatican II," defense of orthodoxy or "aggiornomento," purity of doctrine or healthy pluralism. We have seen the evil of Christians persecuting other Christians in their blasphemous defense of religion as they conceive it. Christian love cannot be divided between many objects, but united on God alone. Our efforts in this direction, recommended in the *Ascent,* establish the need for an integration of affection in a united dedication to the Lord. "The strength of the soul…is ruled by the will. When the will directs these faculties, passions, and appetites toward God…, the soul preserves its strength for God, and comes to love him with all its might" (A, 3, 16, 2).

John's way of love is set out in greater detail in the *Spiritual Canticle* and the *Living Flame of Love.* The former describes the dynamism and stages of love, while the latter addresses the fullness and satisfaction of union. The first thirty-one stanzas of the *Canticle* were written by John when in prison in Toledo, and thus the poem is in a sense autobiographical, "composed in a love flowing from abundant mystical understanding" (C, Prologue, 2). The journey of love, like that of faith, leads to profound knowledge of God. John calls it "mystical wisdom" and claims that "it is given according to the mode of faith, through which we love God without understanding him" (*ibid.*).

As John himself explains (C, 22, 3), the *Canticle* presents the stages of the journey of love:

> 1. a period of anxious search for the loved one, in which one learns a lot about the Beloved, acquiring partial knowledge that serves to arouse one's impatient desire (C, 1–12);
> 2. an initial encounter with the Beloved, leading to the love of espousal, but still filled with preoccupations (C, 13–21);
> 3. the experience of total union in spiritual marriage, with all the love that results (C, 22–35);
> 4. the yearning for transformation in a glorious final union (C, 36–40).

The journey begins with the awareness that the loved one is hidden deep within oneself, and must be sought with love (C, 1, 6). The initial encounter is a visit from the Lord "with strong love amid the intense loving desires" the seeker has previously shown (C, 13, 2). The spiritual marriage is "a total transformation...in which each surrenders the entire possession of self to the other" (C, 22, 3). Finally, each yearns to become more like the other in mutual transformation (C, 36, 3).

The journey of love is both the deepening of the human experience of love of God and the revelation of God's loving action in the individual. In the journey of faith we saw that knowledge of God is rectified through the two purifications, conceptual and vital. In the journey of love our experience of God's presence is purified in three ways. First, we love God in God's apparent absence. When God seems to withdraw to purify a person's love, the individual learns to appreciate the transcendence of God. As we often think of a distant friend, so an individual thinks of the "distant" Lord and experiences presence in absence. "The soul, enamored of the Word, her Bridegroom, the Son of God, longs for union with him," and "records her longings of love and complains to him of his absence" (C, 1, 2). Such a person, having broken false attachments, still must suffer the apparent absence of the loved one.[72]

Second, we love God in union. Here we experience God's love and goodness and under this challenging illumination see God in everything. This is the genuine knowledge by participation. "The soul relates the sovereign favor God granted by recollecting her in the intimacy of his love, which is the union with God, or transformation, through love" (C, 26, 2).

The third way of purifying one's experience of God's presence is through a sense of absence, of a lack within ourselves, in the very experience of union. Present to God, we see our own weakness and imperfections, and anxiety at our insufficiencies leads to a feeling of absence even though God is actually present to us.

The love of God is a transforming experience in a loving union.[73] "This spiritual marriage...is a total transformation in the Beloved, in which each surrenders the entire possession of self to the other with a certain consummation of the union of love" (C, 22, 3). This transforming union causes all the faculties of an individual to be moved under the direction of God (F, 2, 34), seeking always to function in union with God (C, 27, 7). It is also an illuminating experience, "for true and perfect love knows not how to keep anything hidden from the beloved" (C, 23, 1).

The journey of love is a courageous undertaking that leads to the possession of God through a loving union that transforms our whole approach to life and grants a participation in the life of God. "In the union and transformation of love each gives possession of self to the other, and each leaves and exchanges self for the other. Thus each one lives in the other and is the other, and both are one in the transformation of love" (C, 12, 7). The journey is rigorously demanding, and the gradual purification of love is a serious endeavor. "This is acquired through complete mortification of all the vices and appetites of one's own nature" (F, 2, 32). It leads to the total possession of God, and everything else in divine union, as the "Prayer of a Soul Taken With Love" explains: "all things are mine; and God himself is mine and for me, because Christ is mine and all for me" (Sayings, 27).

John's way of love, then, complements and completes the way of faith. In reality, these two ways are simply different aspects of the one journey, the one plan God has imprinted in the depths of each person. Both progressively reveal God to us.

Experiencing God

John of the Cross sought to encounter God in various ways during his early life, but soon concluded that partial contacts leave us profoundly dissatisfied (A, 2, 4, 3). The soul, searching for her spouse in the *Canticle*, expresses what became John's own response. "My Lord, my Spouse, you have given yourself to me partially; now may you give me yourself completely.... You have communicated by means of others, as if joking with me; now may you do so truly, communicating yourself by yourself" (C, 6, 6). John's understanding of God is based on a rich synthesis of the Christian heritage, to which he adds his own penetrating intuitions. His beautiful "Romances" portray the vision of the eternal life of God, the shared love in the intercommunications of the Trinity, their love-filled gift of creation, the incarnation, and the redeeming ministry of the Lord. The history of salvation is presented as a project of love, overflowing from the Trinity's inner life of love. Rich in doctrine, the "Romances" are an excellent example of how the content of faith becomes alive, and life-giving, in the believer's spirituality. John's appreciation of salvation history is again portrayed in the beautiful poem, "For I know well the spring." This is a personal meditation on God's providential care and love, written while in prison.

John detaches himself from all finite images of God, whether provided by philosophy, theology, popular piety, or spiritual experiences, and he commits himself to the God of our faith. "For God is the substance and concept of faith, and faith is the secret and the mystery. And when that which faith covers and hides from us is revealed…then the substance and mysteries of the secrets will be uncovered to the soul" (C, 1, 10). Confidently, John affirms that "faith…gives and communicates God himself to us" (C, 12, 4).

Faith, the guide to union, "lies beyond all this understanding, taste, feeling, and imagining" (A, 2, 4, 2), challenging us to abide in total darkness, since this alone prepares us for union with God. Rooted in faith, John, like all mystics, is also convinced that God wishes to reveal the divine presence to those believers who seek union. In the *Canticle,* John presents three modes of divine presence: first is the presence by essence (God sustaining all creation); second is the presence of grace (God living in those who have not rejected the divine self-gift); third is the mystical presence, which includes a deeper appreciation of the other two (C, 11, 3–4). This is the richest. John presents this mystical presence as a secret indwelling of God, of which some individuals become aware as God from time to time communicates knowledge and love to them (F, 4, 14).

John purifies all false images of God, confidently gives himself to the God of faith, and is convinced that individuals can receive deeper experiences of God's presence. Like other mystics, John shares with us his experience, as well as he can, fully aware that "not even they who receive these communications" are able to "describe…the understanding [God] gives to loving souls in whom he dwells" (C, Prologue, 1).

We know God principally through the divine attributes, those qualities of God identified by the church from the reflections of philosophy, Scripture, theology, and religious experience. Philosophers may typically trace the root of these attributes in the one divine nature, but Christian mystics often associate them with the Trinity of divine persons. "Each of these attributes is the very being of God in his one and only suppositum, which is the Father, the Son, and the Holy Spirit" (F, 3, 2).

John speaks about the ineffable revelation of God in certain contemplative experiences and declares, "God is the direct object of this knowledge in that one of his attributes (his omnipotence, fortitude, goodness, sweetness, and so on) is sublimely experienced" (A, 2, 26, 3). He adds that anyone who thus experiences God finds it impossible to explain the experience to others. It seems that such a person experiences God's attributes *vitally*, encountering God as goodness, fortitude, and so on. This revelation produces "incomparable delight." The individual becomes aware that "God in his unique and simple being is all the power and grandeur of his attributes" (F, 3, 2).

John lists the divine attributes in both the *Ascent* (omnipotence, fortitude, goodness, and sweetness, etc.) and the *Living Flame* (almighty, wise, and good, merciful, just, powerful, and loving, etc.). He says that "although at times individuals use words in reference to this knowledge, they clearly realize that they have said nothing of what they experienced, for no term can give adequate expression to it" (A, 2, 26, 4). John lists traditional attributes, and although he ends each list with "etc." he never specifies any new attributes. In fact, he adds that "God is the other infinite attributes and powers of which we have no knowledge" (F, 3, 2). Probably John's profound experience is a deeper appreciation of the attributes we already know. Even in times of profound union and special illumination, John speaks about the fundamental mysteries of the Incarnation and Redemption. "In this high state of spiritual marriage the Bridegroom reveals his wonderful secrets to the soul," principally communicating "sweet mysteries of his Incarnation and the ways of the redemption of humankind" (C, 23, 1). When later describing a person's desire to pass to a life of glory, he says the person yearns to

be with Christ so as "to see him face to face and thoroughly understand the profound and eternal mysteries of his Incarnation" (C, 37,
1). Thus, even the most profound experiences seem to be deeper
penetrations of truths known from revelation. Although John the
mystic seeks to communicate the mystical knowledge he has received, he gives us the traditional attributes of God, adding no new
ones, but indicating by his enthusiasm and awe that he has pen-
etrated the meaning of these attributes more profoundly than
people usually do, and that he somehow *experiences* the attributes
rather than merely *understanding* them in the abstract.

One attribute, God's beauty, is very special for John. He uses
this word to describe God, always using the noun form *hermosura*
(beauty) rather than the adjective *hermoso* (beautiful). This unusual
description is not used analogically from the beauty of nature, but
rather is clearly intended to refer to the inner being of God. He
describes the seeker in the *Canticle* deliberately asking God "to show
her his beauty, his divine essence" (C, 11, 2), so that the person may
granted "a certain spiritual feeling of his presence" and "some deep
glimpses of his divinity and beauty" (C, 11, 1). For John "beauty" is
a divine attribute equivalent to the divine essence itself. Other theologians and saints use the justice, or love, or being of God as their
supreme category, but John proclaims God's "beauty."

In two passages John seems swept off his feet when he thinks
of God's beauty. In one, quoted earlier, he uses the word twenty-four
times in a single paragraph (C, 36, 5), and in the other six times in
four lines (C, 11, 10). Madre Francisca de la Madre de Dios testified
that on one of his visits to Beas, sometime in 1582–1584, John was
carried away by the thought of God's beauty and wrote five additional stanzas of the *Canticle* on the beauty of God (36–40). Commentators on the lives of mystics refer to the constant repetition of
a concept as mystical obsession. Certainly, John seems so obsessed
with the thought of God's beauty, that it could be part of his own
original direct experience of God.

The word *hermosura* (beauty) is an unusual word in Spanish,
and John typically uses it, not to describe external beauty, but to
point to the beauty of God's inner being. His use is metaphysical, or
transcendent, and it includes the sense of harmony. He speaks of

the soul experiencing "the supreme good and beauty," and refers to it as "his beauty, his divine essence" (C, 11, 1–2).

The entire system of John centers on God, the principal agent in the spiritual life. God draws people to divine life, taking the initiative in every stage of the journey. God's love precedes all human response; it is a love that calls, purifies, illumines, supports in pain, shares, transforms, and unites. God's special interventions in believers' lives are extraordinary, but John's emphasis is not on the extraordinary, even though he is more aware of it than most people. Rather, John steps back from all the wonderful interventions of God, and from the depth of affection the Lover constantly shows, and focuses on the divine characteristics frequently found in the Scriptures.

He stresses four basic qualities of God. First, God is master of the divine self-communication and divine gifts. No matter the stage of spiritual life, or the readiness of the individual, no one can control or effect the transforming graces of the Lord. "For God grants them to whom he wills and for the reason he wills" (A, 2, 32, 2). At times God may have established conditions before certain events take place, but "he will remain silent about the condition" (A, 2, 20, 5). Individuals must respect God's sovereign will and transcendence. "God is above the heavens and speaks from the depths of eternity; we on this earth are blind and understand only the ways of the flesh and of time" (A, 2, 20, 5). When God grants his graces, the individual will find that "there is no reason, or possibility of a reason, why God should look at and exalt her, but that this reason is only in God" (C, 33, 2). Some are led to contemplation, but not others. "Why? He best knows" (N, 1, 9, 9). God is absolute Lord, and sovereignly acts as God wills.

Second, God loves and gives without measure. "The power and the tenacity of love is great, for love captures and binds God himself" (C, 32, 1). Thus in moments of contemplative union God communicates his gifts with loving liberality (C, 27, 1). The hand of the omnipotent Father is "as generous and bountiful as it is powerful and rich" (F, 2, 16). Although sovereign Lord, God participates in a mutual surrender and loving self-gift with those who are drawn to union. Since God loves so much, the believer's response must also be love. "When God is loved he very readily answers the requests of his lover…. Nothing is obtained from God except by love" (C, 1, 13).

The third quality of God is that love leads God to adapt to each person's situation, just as a loving parent treats each child as special. Sometimes, "God accordingly condescends to some souls, granting what is not the best for them" (A, 2, 21, 3). At times, individuals insist on their selfish desires, and "God, though angered, condescends in this and many other ways to the desires of souls" (A, 2, 21, 7). This becomes a dangerous situation, since God may grant a gift that an individual would be better off without. God's love leads to persistent divine effort to draw individuals away from their childish behavior (F, 3, 66).

The fourth quality of God, a basic feature of John's spiritual vision, is God's commitment to the sacramental economy of the church. "Thus God is not inclined to work miracles. When he works them he does so, as they say, out of necessity" (A, 3, 31, 9). Thus, John directs his readers away from the exceptional, preternatural gifts and urges a dedication to the basic ecclesial plan of God. His insistence becomes firm and blunt when he declares, "On judgement day, God will punish the faults and sins of many with whom he communed familiarly here below and to whom he imparted much light and power" (A, 2, 22, 15). John then encourages those individuals who receive unusual experiences to reveal everything to their spiritual directors.

God, sovereign Lord, who loves and gives without measure, adapts to each one's circumstances, and does so most clearly through salvation history in Christ and in the church, where God can repeat "I have already told you all things in my Word, my Son and…I have no other word" (A, 2, 22, 5).

Seeking God, we journey in faith and in love. Those privileged to see the Lord's special presence experience the divine attributes and catch a glimpse of Beauty. Having led us through the rigors of the nights, John brings everyone full circle to focus on the centrality of Jesus and his presence to the church.

CONCLUSION

John of the Cross's "Sketch of the Mount" is a fine synthesis of his system. He says that God is pleased to dwell on this mountain where there remains only the honor and glory of God. However, this spiritual mountain is fertile and fruitful in the lives of those who arrive at the summit. In fact, it is like a perpetual banquet for those who have sought to decrease all self-seeking in their lives. Insofar as they have done so, they now find personal fulfillment. Having absolutized nothing, they now lack nothing. Having desired nothing, they now enjoy everything without even seeking it. The summit is filled with rewards for those who by means of nothing sought everything and found it in God. The gifts and fruits of the Holy Spirit, together with the theological and cardinal virtues, are the new energies in the disciples' lives.

John is an outstanding theologian with a fine grasp of Scripture, systematic theology, and spiritual direction. While his fundamental message is in the poems, his explanations of them are so concrete, and so well-organized, that they are very helpful for those who want to undertake the same journey. John's ideal of holiness focuses on God, but also arrives at the human ideal of integration. His method is simple but rigorous. A mountaineer who has frequently climbed the same peak knows that some ways up succeed and some do not, but after several climbs knows also how to conserve energy, when to eat and drink, and when to abstain, and so on. We respect mountaineers because they get to the peaks, although we know they also paid a price in training and in the sacrifices of the climb. John succeeded but he was also willing to pay the price. If anyone focuses only on the necessary training and denial they have the wrong perspective. John succeeded where so many others turned back or chose lower peaks to climb. John challenges contemporary men and women to keep their eyes on the high peak of Mount Carmel and not to accept a reduced ideal of their call to union.

John attained his goal while immersed in a very busy life, with many administrative and formational responsibilities. Even among full-time ministers today, whether clergy, religious, or laity, few have as many responsibilities—administrative, professional, literary, directional, and ministerial—as John did. Such responsibilities offer no serious obstacle to a singleminded dedication to growth in the life of prayer.[74] Contemplation is not distinct from normal life, nor can it grow out of a dull, uneventful existence. John's full life provided an excellent basis for deeper prayer.

John is a wonderful teacher, well-worthy of the title "Mystical Doctor," since he evidences a superior ability to articulate his vision and challenge. Thus, he challenges others, but also shows the concrete steps to take to arrive at the summit. His works are like handbooks for spiritual directors, or self-help "how-to" books for those who are without adequate spiritual guides in their neighborhood or region.

John is a spiritual prophet that our own generation could well heed. The post-Vatican II church has seen so much theological warfare over different images of institutions, authority structures, rituals, church architecture, formalities of religious life, and incidentals of clerical life. There has been little debate on essentials, and we have even suffered schism over externals. John warned over and over again that the main obstacles to growth in prayer and the spiritual life are *religious* issues to which individuals become attached, self-deluded into thinking that the trivia of religious externals are essential to Christian faith.

John's dealings with the papal, royal, and congregational representatives, together with his careful use of discernment (of critical issues in his own life or in the lives of others), shows that he is no fundamentalist regarding any sources of religious authority, absolutizing neither authority structures nor experience. A skillful interpreter of the movements of the Spirit, he is humble but independent, obedient but co-responsible, rooted in faith and ready to interpret it.

John is a person whose Christian calling is his absorbing destiny. Totally dedicated to achieving his calling, John shows contemporary Christians what fidelity really implies. Neither coddled by the comforts of religion, nor oppressed by its negative forces, John of the Cross attained greatness and prophetically calls generations to follow the path he took.

NOTES

1. See the complete address in Marcelino Menéndez Pelayo, *La Mística Española* (Madrid: Afrodisio Aguado, 1956), pp. 139–201, especially pp. 182–187.

2. The family's struggles and the hardship of life in Spain at that time are described by Crisógono de Jesús, *The Life of St. John of the Cross* (New York: Harper and Brothers, 1958), pp. 2–8; and Federico Ruiz et al., *God Speaks in the Night* (Washington, DC: ICS Publications, 1991), chs. 1–2.

3. Among other lecturers in theology at Salamanca in John's time were Mancio de Corpus Christi (successor to Melchor Cano), Juan de Guevara, Gregorio Gallo, his successor Gaspar de Grajal, and Cristóbal Vela. According to the Carmelite legislation then in effect, besides the university courses John would also have attended classes at home in the monastery of the Carmelite college of San Andrés, on the great masters of the Order, John Baconthorpe and Michael of Bologna. See Bruno de Jésus-Marie, *St. John of the Cross* (New York: Sheed and Ward, 1932), pp. 30–31; and Ruiz, et al., *God Speaks*, pp. 76–78, 90–91.

4. The few known details of John's life during his time in Salamanca are given in Crisógono, *Life*, pp. 37–40; Ruiz, et al., *God Speaks*, ch. 3.

5. Teresa refers to this meeting in *The Book of Her Foundations*, ch. 3.

6. Teresa will say, of his readiness this new life: "As for Father Fray John of the Cross, no trial was necessary. Even though he had lived among the calced friars, those of the cloth, he always lived a life of great perfection and religious observance" (*Foundations*, 13, 1).

7. See *Foundations*, ch. 13.

8. A description of their way of life and penances is given in *Foundations*, ch. 14.

9. See Crisógono, *Life, p. 64.*

10. Stories of John's successes and struggles for acceptance at the Incarnation are found in Crisógono, *Life*, pp. 73–77; and Ruiz, et al., *God Speaks*, ch. 5.

11. Crisógono de Jesús acknowledges that there were some grounds for the displeasure of the Ancient Observance. After all, they authorized the

reform and supported its early ventures, but later they were ignored and bypassed, as different authorities began to prefer and support the discalced. See Crisógono, *Life*, p. 87. For a sympathetic account of the position of the Carmelite Order in the face of the excesses of the discalced and others, see especially Joachim Smet, *The Carmelites: A History of the Brothers of Our Lady of Mount Carmel*, vol. 2, *The Post Tridentine Period, 1550–1600* (Darien, IL: Carmelite Spiritual Center, 1976), chs. 1–4.

12. Teresa, who had been informed of the imprisonment of John soon after it occurred, wrote to Philip II on December 4, 1577 asking for his intervention. However, John's whereabouts was still a mystery to Teresa a month later. She continued to work for John's release, writing not only to Philip II, but also to anyone who could help, including Gracián, and Ana de los Angeles, prioress of the discalced nuns in Toledo.

13. For a detailed description of John's imprisonment, see Crisógono, *Life*, ch. 9, and Ruiz, et al., *God Speaks*, ch. 6. For a correlation of those events with appropriate passages in John's writings, see Bruno, *St. John of the Cross*, ch. 13.

14. John was rector in Baeza from 1579–82. For the events of those years, including the death of John's mother, Catalina Alvarez, see Crisógono, *Life*, pp.141–151; Ruiz, et al., *God Speaks*, ch. 7.

15. For a fine presentation of Nicolás de Jesús-María Doria, see chapter 18 in Bruno, *St. John of the Cross*, pp. 384–312. Like many religous leaders before him and since, Fr. Doria was a rigorist who thought his concentration of power would preserve the reform. Referring to his teachings, some listeners suggested that "not only the flock, but the shepherds themselves were frozen with terror." Others referred to "Doria's pharisaism." For a more sympathetic portrayal of Doria, see Joachim Smet, *The Carmelites*, vol. 2, *The Post Tridentine Period*, ch. 4.

16. Two of John's letters from this period give some idea of how he felt and with what resignation and good spirits he approached his mistreatment. See letter 25 to Ana de Jesús and letter 26 to María de la Encarnación, both dated July 6, 1591.

17. For a summary of the life and teachings of this dedicated follower of Teresa, see chapter 6, "Jeronimo Gracián," in E. Allison Peers, *Studies of the Spanish Mystics*, vol. 2 (London: SPCK, 1960), pp. 117–148.

18. Besides Teresa's writings, our primary sources for biographical information on John of the Cross are the manuscripts and testimonies collected during the canonical processes leading to his beatification and canonization. Some of these documents are in the Vatican archives of the Sacred Congregation of Rites, and others in Madrid's National Library. Fr. Crisógono lists them and specifies the content of each in his *Life*, pp. 314–318.

19. The best description of John of the Cross's appearance and personality comes from Fr. Eliseo de los Mártires, who knew John for many years

and lived with him for several years at Granada. Crisógono presents and expands on this verbal portrait in his *Life,* ch. 21.

20. Compare Segundo Galilea, *The Future of Our Past: The Spanish Mystics Speak to Contemporary Spirituality* (Notre Dame, IN: Ave Maria Press, 1985); Leonard Doohan, "The Contemporary Significance of the Life and Works of John of the Cross," *Studies in Formative Spirituality* 13 (1992): 9-17.

21. These are probably not John's first writings, but they are the first that survive. Some witnesses refer to compositions, now lost, from the early periods of John's novitiate in Medina del Campo, his university studies in Salamanca, his time in Duruelo when the first constitutions of the discalced friars were drawn up, and his term as chaplain at the Incarnation in Avila.

22. John read and studied a lot. Witnesses speak of his interest in St. Augustine, his constant use of the monasteries' libraries, and of course his absorbing interest in and dedication to the Bible. He was a fine and valued theologian. John explicitly quotes or mentions Aristotle, Ovid, Dionysius the Areopagite, Augustine, Gregory the Great, Thomas Aquinas, Bernard, Boethius, Boscán, and Teresa of Avila. Elsewhere he seems indirectly influenced by Baconthorpe, Tauler, Ruysbroeck, and popular songs and poems of his day. See Crisógono, *Life,* p. 227.

23. This is also true of his prose style. Kavanaugh observes that "it is not apparent that he took pains to polish his prose. His sentences can get complicated, repetitious, and cluttered. Not infrequently, however, the inspiration of his poetry overflows into his prose, offering passages of literary power, originality, and beauty." See "General Introduction" to the 1991 revised edition of the *Collected Works,* p. 34.

24. For a fine approach to John's use of Scripture and his theological insight, see *John of the Cross: Selected Writings,* ed. Kieran Kavanaugh (New York: Paulist Press, 1987), pp. 24–34.

25. If John is to speak to us today we must reinterpret his writings in the light of Vatican II, and not from an older Jansenistic perspective as damaging to his vision as it is inaccurate. Like all mystics, John's work needs an appropriate hermeneutic to make it accessible and challenging to modern seekers for union with God.

26. In addition to the speech of Menéndez Pelayo, quoted above, see Dámaso Alonso, *La Poesía de San Juan de la Cruz* (Madrid: Aguilar, 1942).

27. Both John and Teresa have a poem on the same theme, "I live, but not in myself." This could be an example of such devotional competitions.

28. See Gerald Brenan, *St. John of the Cross: His Life and Poetry* (Cambridge: University Press, 1973), pp. 104–111; also Bernard McGarty, "Images from Nature in the Spiritual Canticle of St. John of the Cross," *Spiritual Life* 25 (1979): 166–175.

29. As mentioned above, Teresa of Avila wrote a poem with the same first line and similar themes. If these are two independent poems and not the product of devotional competition nor the result of later copyists' confusion, then Teresa possibly wrote hers seven years earlier.

30. See George M. Anderson, "Maxims as a Source for Prayer," *Contemplative Review* 14 (Summer 1981): 10–13.

31. See the facsimile edition available in San Juan de la Cruz, *Dichos de Luz y Amor: Edición facsimil (Codice de Andújar)*, ed. José Vicente Rodriguez (Madrid: Editorial de Espiritualidad, 1976).

32. See Judy B. McInnis, "Eucharistic and Conjugal Symbolism in The Spiritual Canticle of Saint John of the Cross," *Renascence* 36 (1984): 118–138.

33. See Kavanaugh's detailed outline of both works, together with the introductory notes, on pages 101–109 and 353–357 of the 1991 revised ICS edition of John's *Collected Works*.

34. In the *Spiritual Canticle* treatise, John fulfills his promise (Prologue, 4) to develop the commentary stanza by stanza and verse by verse. Elsewhere he is not so consistent. The *Ascent,* for example, begins as a commentary on the "Dark Night" poem, devoting 13 chapters to the first line, chapter 14 to the second line, and chapter 15 to the rest of the first stanza. Book II announces the second stanza, but then John makes no further references to the poem in the rest of the *Ascent.* The *Dark Night* treatise takes a similar approach to the first two stanzas of the same poem, but simply presents the third stanza and comments on its first line before breaking off abruptly, leaving the other five stanzas without commentary.

35. John made numerous breviary-sized copies of the helpful diagram that precedes the *Ascent,* though all of them have been lost except a notarized copy of the one used by Magdalena del Espíritu Santo, which differs significantly from later stylized versions used in printed editions of John's works. This has led to some debate about the details of the sketch. Does John mean to suggest, for example, that the side paths are complete dead-ends (as one might conclude from the copy of Magdalena del Espíritu Santo), or does he believe that they do eventually reach the summit, albeit by a circuitous route (as in some artists' renderings, possibly influenced by other original copies now lost)? For more on the sketch of the Mount, see E. W. Trueman Dicken, *The Crucible of Love: A Study of the Mysticism of St. Teresa of Jesus and St. John of the Cross* (New York: Sheed & Ward, 1963), pp. 237–244; Ruiz, et al., *God Speaks,* pp. 213–215.

36. For a recent English-language discussion of the two versions of the poem and its commentary, see Colin P. Thompson, *The Poet and the Mystic: A Study of the Cántico Espiritual of San Juan de la Cruz* (New York: Oxford University Press, 1977).

37. Many commentators consider the *Spiritual Canticle* the most suitable book to give first-time readers of John. See Michael Dodd, "Beginners and the Spiritual Canticle: a Reflection," *Spiritual Life* 29 (1983): 195–208.

38. For more on the Living Flame and Doña Ana de Peñalosa, see Ruiz, et al., *God Speaks,* pp. 246-249, 278-281, 323-325.

39. See Barnabas Ahern, "The Use of Scripture in the Spiritual Theology of John of the Cross," *Catholic Biblical Quarterly* 14 (1952): 6–17.

40. Note that, in the terminology of that time, "mystical theology" refers to the contemplative experience of God in prayer, not to the academic study of mysticism.

41 See chapter 9 in Brenan, *St. John of the Cross,* especially pp. 118–137.

42. See Capistran J. Haas, "Saint John of the Cross: Poet," *Spiritual Life* 28 (1982): 219–225.

43. All of John's poems, except the romances and "A lone young shepherd," begin in the first person. They are all in some sense autobiographical, even the dialogue in the "Spiritual Canticle."

44. See Gabriel of St. Mary Magdalen, *St. John of the Cross: Doctor of Divine Love and Contemplation* (Westminster, MD: Newman Press, 1954), p. 1, where the author, summarizing John's teaching as "the way of love," speaks about "the profound unity of the work of St. John of the Cross," identifying "a single doctrinal line running through all his works," and suggesting that "the Saint has done nothing else but mark out for us the road which leads to the perfection of the life of love."

45. The bulk of St. Teresa's teaching on prayer is found in her three most famous works. The *Way of Perfection* describes for her nuns the fundamental virtues needed for the spiritual journey, and focuses especially on the early stages of prayer. Written for her spiritual director to give an account of her own journey and unusual prayer experiences, the *Book of Her Life* deals more extensively with growth in contemplation; in chapters 11-22, Teresa interrupts the narrative of her life with a long digression on four successive stages of prayer (which she calls meditation, prayer of quiet, sleep of the faculties, and union) compared allegorically with four ways of watering a garden (the classic "four waters"). But the Saint's most mature presentation is found in the *Interior Castle,* where she describes the spiritual journey in terms of an inner pilgrimage through seven progressively more interior "dwelling places" to the center of one's soul, where God alone dwells. In any case, Teresa's teaching on the stages of prayer is in some ways more difficult to systematize than John's, since she rethinks some of her distinctions and terminology from work to work as her experience grows.

46. See Gabriel of St. Mary Magdalen, "The Demands of Love," in *St. John of the Cross,* pp. 21–43.

47. Closely linked to this patience is gentleness. See Thomas Kane, "Gentleness in John of the Cross," Parts 1–3, *Contemplative Review* 14 (Winter 1981): 1–8; 15 (Spring 1982): 20–24; 15 (Summer 1982): 14–19.

48. This journey can be seen as the Christian participation in the the cross of Christ, so well explained by Edith Stein (Sr. Teresa Benedicta of the Cross), the Carmelite nun of Jewish ancestry killed in the gas chambers of Auschwitz in early August, 1942. See Edith Stein, *The Science of the Cross: A Study of St. John of the Cross* (London: Burns and Oates, 1960).

49. The focus of John's work is conditioned by the people he encounters in his own ministry, frequently nuns of the reform who had already dedicated themselves to the spiritual journey; he could challenge them

perhaps more vigorously than he would true beginners. Demanding on himself, John was very senstitive to others and gentle with their struggles.

50. For an overview of these two nights and the relationship of love and suffering during this experience, see Gabriel of St. Mary Magdalen, "The Sufferings of Love," in *St. John of the Cross*, pp. 44–67.

51. For more on the nature of contemplation and the spiritual director's task in helping directees attain it, see Gabriel of St. Mary Magdalen, "Acquired Contemplation," in *St. John of the Cross*, pp. 100–124; see also Joel Giallanza, "Spiritual Direction According to St. John of the Cross," *Contemplative Review* 11 (Fall 1978): 31–37.

52. Here I have combined the slightly different versions of the classic "three signs" that John presents in chapters 13 to 15 of Book Two of the Ascent, chapter 9 of Book One of the Night, and *Sayings*, 119. For more on the "three signs," see Gabriel of St. Mary Magdalene, *The Spiritual Director According to the Principles of St. John of the Cross* (Westminster, MD: Newman Press, 1951) pp. 51–53; Trueman Dicken, *Crucible of Love*, pp. 145–152, 159–161.

53. See David Center, "Christian Freedom and The Nights of St. John of the Cross," *Carmelite Studies* 2 (1982): 3–80.

54. Compare Karol Wojtyla (Pope John Paul II), *Faith According to St. John of the Cross* (San Francisco: Ignatius Press, 1981); "The Question of Faith in St. John of the Cross," *Carmelite Studies* 2 (1982): 223–273.

55. For further clarification of the individual's feelings at this time, see Joel Giallanza, "Weariness in the Spiritual Life," *Spiritual Life* 29 (1983): 10–17; Denys Turner, "St. John of the Cross and Depression," *Downside Review* 106 (1988): 157–180; and Maria Edwards, "Depression Or Dark Night?" *Contemplative Review* 18 (1985): 34–37.

56. John's view of the relationship between night and light has a paschal dimension: he sees the spiritual life as a true exodus. See John Sullivan, "Night and Light: The Poet John of the Cross and the 'Exultet' of the Easter Liturgy," *Ephemerides Carmeliticae* 27 (1976): 453–488.

57. See Leonard Doohan, "Personal Fulfillment in the Life and Teachings of St. John of the Cross," *Living Prayer* (1988): 28–32.

58. See Stein, *Science of the Cross*, pp. 140–207.

59. See Paul T. Russell, "The Humanity of Christ in St. John of the Cross," *Spiritual Life* 30 (1984): 143–156.

60. Russell, p. 155, says: "In John of the Cross, the Humanity of the Word-Made-Flesh is not a concession which mystics are forced to make to orthodoxy. On the contrary, it is the Door by which we shall receive those special goods in the day of eternal bliss."

61. See "Anthropology," in *St. John of the Cross: Selected Writings*, ed. Kieran Kavanaugh, pp. 34–37.

62. For John's positive approach to all creation, see Camille Anne Campbell, "Creation-Centered Carmelites: Teresa and John," *Spiritual Life* 28 (1982): 15–25; and Leslie Lund, "Carmel and World Transformation," *Spiritual Life* 29 (1983): 97–105.

63. While John insists that nothing should come between ourselves and God, he believes that every positive human value should be integrated into a God-centered life. As an example of his approach, see Michael Dodd, "Saint John of the Cross and Friendship," *Spiritual Life* 26 (1980): 194–204.

64. See Joel Giallanza, "Myths of Detachment," *Spiritual Life* 27 (1981): 210–218.

65. For John's understanding of desire, see Leslie Lund, "Desire in St. John of the Cross," *Spiritual Life* 31 (1985): 83–100.

66. See Michael Dodd, "Divinization in John of the Cross," *Spiritual Life* 24 (1978): 258–263.

67. See Mary Pellicane, "The Spiritual Journey," *Contemplative Review* 9 (1976): 17–21.

68. See Richard P Hardy, "Fidelity to God in the Mystical Experience of Fray Juan de la Cruz," *Eglise et Théologie* 11 (1980): 57–75.

69. See Deirdre Green, "St. John of the Cross and Mystical Unknowing," *Religious Studies* 22 (1986): 29–40.

70. For an analysis of John's appreciation of emptiness and solitude, see Richard P. Hardy, "Solitude: A Sanjuanist Perspective," *Eglise et Théologie* 6 (1975): 5–23.

71. In chapters 18 to 20 in Book Two of the Dark Night, borrowing the image of a mystical ladder from earlier authors, John describes ten steps in God's purification of a person's life through love, ten steps that lead to the redirection of life under the guidance of the Holy Spirit. See Michael Griffin, "The Ladder of Love of St. John of the Cross," *Spiritual Life* 29 (1983): 3–9.

72. See Gilbert Padilla, "The Hidden Beloved One," *Spiritual Life* 30 (1984): 174–176.

73. See Mary Paul Cutri, "The Touch of God: Human/Divine Intimacy," *Spiritual Life* 30 (1984): 157–162.

74. See Leonard Doohan, "John of the Cross and the Laity," *Spiritual Life* 39 (1993): 164–174.

Select Bibliography of
Works Related to John of the Cross

Ahern, Barnabas. "The Use of Scripture in the Spiritual Theology of St. John of the Cross." *Catholic Biblical Quarterly* 14 (1952): 6–17.

Alonso, Dámaso. *La Poesía de San Juan de la Cruz.* Madrid: Aguilar, 1942.

Anderson, George M. "Maxims as a Source for Prayer." *Contemplative Review* 14 (Summer 1981): 10–13.

Balfe, Kathleen Mary. *Thoughts of Saint John of the Cross for Every Day.* New York: Benziger, 1924.

Baruzi, Jean. *Saint Jean de la Croix et le Problème de l'Expérience Mystique.* Paris: Librairie Felix Alcan, 1924.

A Benedictine of Stanbrook Abbey. *Mediaeval Mystical Tradition and Saint John of the Cross.* Westminster, MD: Newman Press, 1954.

Brenan, Gerald. *St. John of the Cross: His Life and Poetry.* Poetry translated by Lynda Nicholson. Cambridge, England: Cambridge University Press, 1973.

Bruno de Jésus-Marie. *St. John of the Cross.* Edited by Benedict Zimmerman. New York: Sheed and Ward, 1932.

Bruno de Jésus-Marie, ed. *Three Mystics: El Greco, St. John of the Cross, St. Teresa of Avila.* London: Sheed and Ward, 1952.

Campbell, Camille Anne. "Creation-Centered Carmelites: Teresa and John." *Spiritual Life* 28 (1982): 15–25.

Center, David. "Christian Freedom and The Nights of St. John of the Cross." *Carmelite Studies* 2 (1982): 3–80.

Collings, Ross. *John of the Cross.* Collegeville, MN: Liturgical Press, Michael Glazier Book, 1990.

Conlon, Dermot. "Synonyms and the World around Us." *Contemplative Review* 19 (Summer 1986): 11–15.

Crisógono de Jesús Sacramentado. *The Life of St. John of the Cross.* Translated by Kathleen Pond. New York: Harper and Brothers, 1958.

Cristiani, Leon. *St. John of the Cross: Prince of Mystical Theology.* Garden City, NY: Doubleday, 1962.

Cugno, Alain. *Saint John of the Cross: Reflections on Mystical Experience.* New York: Seabury Press, 1982.

Culligan, Kevin G. *Toward a Model of Spiritual Direction Based on the Writings of Saint John of the Cross and Carl R. Rogers.* Ph.D. dissertation, Boston University, 1979; Ann Arbor, MI: University Microfilms, 1981.

———. "Mysticism, Transformation and Spiritual Disciplines: the Teachings of St. John of the Cross." *Spiritual Life* 30 (1984): 131–142.

Cutri, Mary Paul. "The Touch of God: Human/Divine Intimacy." *Spiritual Life* 30 (1984): 157–162.

D'Souza, Camillus-Paul. "Poverty and Prayer in St. John of the Cross." *Carmelite Studies* 1 (1980): 204–212.

Dicken, E.W. Trueman. *The Crucible of Love: A Study of the Mysticism of St. Teresa of Jesus and St. John of the Cross.* New York: Sheed and Ward, 1963.

Dodd, Michael. "Divinization in John of the Cross." *Spiritual Life* 24 (1978): 258–263.

———. "Saint John of the Cross and Friendship." *Spiritual Life* 26 (1980): 194–204.

———. "Beginners and the Spiritual Canticle: A Reflection." *Spiritual Life* 29 (1983): 195–208.

Doohan, Leonard. "The Contemporary Significance of the Life and Works of St. John of the Cross." *Studies in Formative Spirituality* 13 (1992): 9-17.

———. "John of the Cross and the Laity." *Spiritual Life* 39 (1993): 164-174.

———. "Personal Fulfillment in the Life and Teachings of St. John of the Cross." *Living Prayer* (January-February 1988): 28–32.

Edwards, Denis. "Experience of God and Explicit Faith: A Comparison of John of the Cross and Karl Rahner." *Thomist* 46 (1982): 33–74.

Edwards, Maria. "Depression or Dark Night?" *Contemplative Review* 18 (Winter 1985): 34–37.

Fischer, Roland. "Interpretation and Meaning of a Visionary Drawing by St. John of the Cross." *Studia Mystica* 3 (1980): 60–73.

Florent, Lucien-Marie. "Spiritual Direction According to St. John of the Cross." *Carmelite Studies* 1 (1980): 3–34.

Frost, Bede. *Saint John of the Cross: An Introduction to His Philosophy, Theology, and Spirituality.* New York: Harper and Bros., 1937.

Gabriel of St. Mary Magdalen. *St. John of the Cross: Doctor of Divine Love and Contemplation.* Translated by a Benedictine of Stanbrook Abbey. Westminster, MD: The Newman Press, 1954.

———. *The Spiritual Director According to the Principles of St. John of the Cross.* Translated by a Benedictine of Stanbrook Abbey. Westminster, MD: Newman Press, 1951.

Galilea, Segundo. *The Future of Our Past: The Spanish Mystics Speak to Contemporary Spirituality.* Notre Dame, IN: Ave Maria Press, 1985.

Garrigou-Lagrange, Reginald. *Christian Perfection and Contemplation According to St. Thomas Aquinas and St. John of the Cross.* Translated by M. Timothea Doyle. St. Louis: Herder, 1946.

Giallanza, Joel. "Spiritual Direction According to St. John of the Cross." *Contemplative Review* 11 (Fall 1978): 31–37.

———. "Myths of Detachment." *Spiritual Life* 27 (1981): 210–218.

———. "Weariness in the Spiritual Life." *Spiritual Life* 29 (1983): 10–17.

Gicovate, Bernard. *St. John of the Cross*. New York: Twayne Publishers, 1971.

Green, Deirdre. "St. John of the Cross and Mystical Unknowing." *Religious Studies* 22 (1986): 29–40.

Gregson, Vernon J. "The Dark Night: a Text and its Contemporary Personal and Social Significance." *Catholic Theological Society of America Proceedings* 39 (1984): 175–181.

Griffin, Michael. "The Ladder of Love of St. John of the Cross." *Spiritual Life* 29 (1983): 3–9.

Haas, Capistran J. "Saint John of the Cross: Poet." *Spiritual Life* 28 (1982): 219–225.

Hardy, Richard P. "Solitude: A Sanjuanist Perspective." *Eglise et Théologie* 6 (1975): 5–23.

———. " 'Silencio Divino': A Sanjuanist Study." *Eglise et Théologie* 7 (1976): 219–233.

———. "Nursing: A Sanjuanist Image." *Science et Esprit* 28 (1976): 297–307.

———. "Early Biographical Documentation on Juan de la Cruz." *Science et Esprit* 30 (1978): 313–323.

———. "A Personality Sketch." *Ephemerides Carmeliticae* 29 (1978): 507–518.

———. "Fidelity to God in the Mystical Experience of Fray Juan de la Cruz." *Eglise et Théologie* 11 (1980): 57–75.

———. *The Search for Nothing: The Life of John of the Cross*. New York: Crossroad, 1982.

Howe, Elizabeth T. "The Crowded Night: the Concatenation of Imagery in the Dark Night of Saint John of the Cross." *Studia Mystica* 8 (1985): 59–69.

———. *Mystical Imagery: Santa Teresa de Jesús and San Juan de la Cruz*. New York: Peter Lang, 1988.

John of the Cross. *The Collected Works of St. John of the Cross*. Translated by Kieran Kavanaugh and Otilio Rodriguez. With Revisions and Introductions by Kieran Kavanaugh. Rev. ed. Washington, DC: ICS Publications, 1991.

———. *The Complete Works of Saint John of the Cross*. Translated and edited by E. Allison Peers, 3 vols. 3rd rev. ed. Westminster, Md.: Newman Press, 1953.

———. *John of the Cross: Selected Writings*. Translated by Kieran Kavanaugh. New York: Paulist Press, 1987.

Kane, Thomas. "Gentleness in John of the Cross." Parts 1–3. *Contemplative Review* 14 (Winter 1981): 1–8; 15 (Spring 1982): 20–24; 15 (Summer 1982): 14–19.

Keller, Joseph. "The Function of Paradox in Mystical Discourse (John of the Cross)." *Studia Mystica* 6 (1983): 3–19.

Kristo, Jure. "The Interpretation of Religious Experience: What Do Mystics Intend When They Talk about their Experience?" *Journal of Religion* 62 (1982): 21–38.

Lund, Leslie. "Carmel and World Transformation." *Spiritual Life* 29 (1983): 97–105.

———. "Desire in St. John of the Cross." *Spiritual Life* 31 (1985): 83–100.

Mallory, Marilyn May. *Christian Mysticism: Transcending Techniques: A Theological Reflection on the Empirical Testing of the Teaching of St. John of the Cross.* Amsterdam: Van Gorcum Assen, 1977.

McGarty, Bernard. "Images from Nature in the Spiritual Canticle of St. John of the Cross." *Spiritual Life* 25 (1979): 166–175.

McInnis, Judy B. "Eucharistic and Conjugal Symbolism in The Spiritual Canticle of Saint John of the Cross." *Renascence* 36 (1984): 118–138.

Nieto, José C. *Mystic, Rebel, Saint: A Study of St. John of the Cross.* Geneva: Librarie Droz, 1979.

O'Donoghue, Noel Dermot. *Mystics for Our Time: Carmelite Meditations for a New Age.* Wilmington, DE: Michael Glazier, 1989.

Pacho, Eulogio. *San Juan de la Cruz y sus Escritos.* Madrid: Ediciones Cristiandad, 1969.

Padilla, Gilbert. "The Hidden Beloved One." *Spiritual Life* 30 (1984): 174–176.

Peers, E. Allison. *Handbook to the Life and Times of St. Teresa and St. John of the Cross.* Westminster, MD: Newman Press, 1954.

———. *Studies of the Spanish Mystics.* Vol. I. New York: Macmillan, 1951. Vol. II. London: SPCK, 1960.

———. *Spirit of Flame: A Study of St. John of the Cross.* Wilton, CT: Morehouse-Barlow Co., 1944 (reprinted 1979).

Pelayo, Menéndez. *La Mística Española.* Madrid: Afrodisio Aguado, 1956.

Pellicane, Mary. "The Spiritual Journey." *Contemplative Review* 9 (Summer 1976): 17–21.

Ruiz Salvador, Frederico. *Introducción a San Juan de la Cruz.* Madrid: BAC, 1968.

———, et al. *God Speaks in the Night: The Life, Times, and Teaching of St. John of the Cross.* Trans. by Kieran Kavanaugh. Washington, DC: ICS Publications, 1991.

Russell, Paul T. "The Humanity of Christ in St. John of the Cross." *Spiritual Life* 30 (1984): 143–156.

Sencourt, Robert. *Carmelite and Poet: A Framed Portrait of St. John of the Cross.* New York: Macmillan, 1944.

Stein, Edith. *The Science of the Cross: A Study of St. John of the Cross.* Edited by L. Gelber and Romaeus Leuven. Translated by Hilda Graef. London: Burns and Oates, 1960.

Streng, Frederick John. "The Ontology of Silence and Comparative Mysticism." *Philosophy Today* 27 (1983): 121–127.

Sullivan, John. "Night and Light: The Poet John of the Cross and the 'Exultet' of the Easter Liturgy." *Ephemerides Carmeliticae* 27 (1976): 453–488.

Tavard, George H. *Poetry and Contemplation in St. John of the Cross.* Athens OH: Ohio University Press, 1988.

Teresa of Avila, St. *The Collected Works of St. Teresa of Avila.* Translated by Kieran Kavanaugh and Otilio Rodriguez. 3 vols. Washington, DC: ICS Publications, 1976–1987.

Thompson, Colin P. *The Poet and the Mystic: A Study of the Cántico Espiritual of San Juan de la Cruz.* Oxford: Oxford University Press, 1977.

Tillyer, Desmond B. *Union with God: The Teaching of St. John of the Cross.* Lincoln, RI: Mowbray, 1984.

Turner, Denys. "St. John of the Cross and Depression." *Downside Review* 106 (1988): 157–170.

Welch, John. *When Gods Die: An Introduction to John of the Cross.* New York: Paulist, 1990.

Wojtyla, Karol. *Faith According to St. John of the Cross.* Translated by Jordan Aumann. San Francisco: Ignatius Press, 1981.

———— "The Question of Faith in St. John of the Cross." *Carmelite Studies* 2 (1982): 223–273.

Zimmerman, Benedict, ed. *St. John of the Cross.* New York: Sheed and Ward, 1932.

The Institute of Carmelite Studies promotes research and publication in the field of Carmelite spirituality. Its members are Discalced Carmelites, part of a Roman Catholic community—friars, nuns and laity—who are heirs to the teaching and way of life of Teresa of Jesus and John of the Cross, men and women dedicated to contemplation and to ministry in the Church and the world. Information concerning their way of life is available through local diocesan Vocation Offices, or from the Vocation Director's Office, 1525 Carmel Road, Hubertus, WI 53033.